THE CHRISTIAN LIFE

AN OWNER'S MANUAL

A Basic Guide to
Spiritual Growth

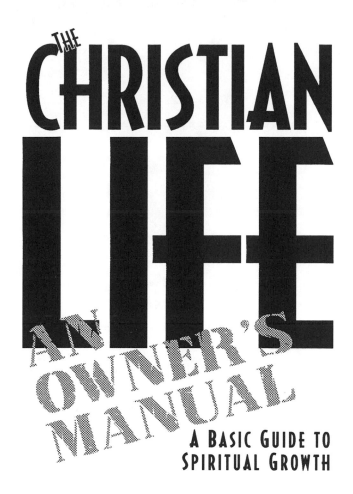

THE CHRISTIAN LIFE

AN OWNER'S MANUAL

A Basic Guide to Spiritual Growth

Scot McCallum

kregel
RESOURCES

Grand Rapids, MI 49501

The Christian Life: An Owner's Manual by Scot McCallum

Copyright © 1995 by Scot McCallum

Published in 1995 by Kregel Resources, an imprint of Kregel Publications, P. O. Box 2607, Grand Rapids, MI 49501. Kregel Resources provides timely and relevant resources for Christian life and service. Your comments and suggestions are valued.

Scripture quotations, unless otherwise noted, are from *The Holy Bible: The New International Version* copyright © 1978 by the International Bible Society. Used by permission of Zondervan Publishing House.

Cover Photograph: Patricia Sgrignoli/POSITIVE IMAGES
Cover and Book Design: Alan G. Hartman

Library of Congress Cataloging-in-Publication Data
McCallum, Scot.
 The Christian life: an owner's manual / Scot McCallum.
  p. cm.
 1. Christian life. I. Title.
BV4501.2.M183 1995   248.4—dc20   95-8344
                     CIP
ISBN 0-8254-3194-8 (paperback)

1 2 3 4 5 Printing / Year 99 98 97 96 95

Printed in the United States of America

CONTENTS

CHAPTER ONE

SIN

People hate this topic

"You're a sinner!" How does it feel to hear that? Now, put a smugly self-righteous face on that accusation, like a preacher or a televangelist. The nerve! The arrogance! Worse yet, think of one of your friends saying this about you! Now do you understand why the Christian message can cause so much offense? No matter how we say it, the message of Christianity tells people they are sinners. So I begin with the topic of sin because it seems like a hard concept to accept.

At the same time, it is the most basic issue in life. We see evidence of human sin everywhere—violence, hate, stealing, lying, abuse—all are graphic demonstrations of the human capacity for personal evil or sin.

We hate to talk about sin, at least in direct terms. Unfortunately, our dread of the topic can lead to ignorance. There are several reasons we don't like to talk about it. For one, nobody likes to discuss their failures. Talking about sin is like talking about our most embarrassing moment, but worse because there are so many sins. We feel uneasy about a topic that might be even darker than we think.

On the other hand, it's foolish to avoid a topic because it's scary. Imagine a doctor who tests you for cancer and then says, "I hate the whole topic of cancer! Let's just pray and try to think positively. Maybe things will work out OK."

The topic of sin is even more loathsome because of the way some Christians have portrayed it. People rave on and on about sin, and then we find out that they're as bad as anyone they ever raged about. It's no surprise that our culture gets excited when a Christian figure falls—it's like watching a bully get beat up!

Finally, to many "sin" means all the things they don't struggle

7

with. It's easy for Christians to call people "sinners" when they're referring to habits that are no temptation for them at all. Someone who never touches a drink will more easily call heavy drinkers sinners. Someone who has always been energetic and motivated may quickly judge lazy people as sinners. This is another reason the term has become associated with self-righteousness and judgment.

With all these bad associations, there are few issues as confusing to Christians as sin. This leads to some real problems. We'll talk about those in a bit. But first, we need to look at God's perspective of sin as it's found in the Bible.

The words for sin

The words for sin in the Bible are the Hebrew word *hat'ah* in the Old Testament and the Greek word *hamartia* in the New Testament. They both basically mean "to miss the mark." So they are metaphorical terms drawn from everyday usage. I could "sin" by missing the trash can with my paper wad. The Bible's writers picked up this imagery to describe human behavior. We often "miss the mark" of God's goodness with our actions or even lack of action.

As the biblical teaching on sin developed, these words came to mean "sin" in a comprehensive sense. The term *hamartia* no longer referred exclusively to the act of sinning but also to a fallen state or a state of corruption. For example, Paul talks in Romans 5:12 about how "sin entered the world through one man" [Adam]. He refers to "sin" as if it were a disease that spread from Adam to everyone else—almost a genetic defect. Later we will consider how sin passes from one person to the whole human race. The point here is the term "sin" can refer to an act, or it can refer to a state—a problem people have.

Falling short of a standard

We could view sin as falling short of a standard. This is probably the most popular understanding of sin. If someone notices I sinned, it usually means I broke some rule. This view of sin is consistent with some passages in the Bible; for example, in Jeremiah 16:10–11, it says:

> "What wrong have we done? What sin have we committed against the Lord our God?" . . . "It is because your fathers forsook me," declares the Lord, "and followed other gods and served and worshiped them. They forsook me and did not keep my law."

Notice especially the last phrase, "They did not keep my law." Here Jeremiah is defining sin as a failure to keep God's law. God's law, recorded in the first five books of the Bible, is surely a standard, and his people sinned by failing to keep it.

Unbelief

Some passages look beneath the violation of a standard; they teach us that sin is an attitude of unbelief. In the Old Testament this was God's biggest problem with the Israelites.

When God brought the Israelites out of the land of Egypt, he intended to guide them into the land he had promised to their forefathers, Abraham, Isaac, and Jacob. Instead, because of conflicts they had with God, he refused to let them enter the Promised Land. They took a forty-year detour, wandering in the wilderness. The problem was their unbelief. God lamented, "How long will they not believe in me, despite all the signs I have performed in their midst?" (Num. 14:11). Belief or unbelief was the main issue between God and his people.

Another revealing incident during that time had to do with Moses, the leader of the Israelites. This episode at Meribah led to his exclusion from the Promised Land. The Israelites had been traveling in the desert for some time, and they were thirsty. Difficulty began when they started to grumble against Moses and God, saying they had been brought out to the wilderness to die. "Why did you bring us into this wilderness? For us and our animals to die out here?" (Num. 20:4). They complained until Moses became angry with them. At God's direction, Moses worked a miracle by striking a rock, and water came out of the rock. When Moses struck the rock he said, "Listen you rebels! Shall we bring forth water for you out of this rock!"

The unexpected thing is that God ultimately became upset with Moses! The people grumbled. They thought God and Moses had brought them out to the wilderness to die. But something about Moses' reaction to their grumbling caused God to say in Numbers 20:12, "Because you did not believe in me to honor me as holy in the sight of the Israelites, you will not bring this community into the land I give them."

The psalmist was amazed at the entire affair. In Psalm 106:32, he notes, "They also provoked [God] to wrath at the waters of Meribah, so that it went hard with Moses on their account." The people provoked God, but Moses wound up in trouble. After delivering them from slavery in Egypt and leading them across the desert, Moses was never allowed to enter the Promised Land!

What was God's problem with Moses? You've already read it—

"Because you did not believe in me!" (Num. 20:12). Was Moses disobedient? Yes. In another passage, Moses' sin is called "rebellion against God's command" (Num. 20:24). Was Moses' sin a deed? An action? Yes. The psalmist describes Moses' sin as "speaking rashly with his lips" (Psalms 106:32–33). Yet at the bottom of it all, the problem was that Moses didn't *believe God.* God's commentary on the situation was, "Because you did not believe me" (Num. 20:12).

What we are seeing here is very important because it reveals how God looks at sin. Specifically, Moses didn't believe in God's goodness. God is so forgiving he wanted to bless the Israelites even though they grumbled at him. Moses, however, spoke a word of judgment to the Israelites—something God never intended. Moses' words misrepresented God's true intent—to give the Israelites what they wanted. This is why God could say Moses didn't believe in him. He didn't believe in God's goodness.

This event was a big deal, both at the time and throughout the rest of the Bible. The seriousness of Moses' offense should be obvious to us. To this day, many are averse to the topic of Christianity because God has been misrepresented to them primarily as the God of judgment and anger! Moses indulged one of the most dangerous and damaging temptations for any leader—to speak angrily when God wants to show compassion.

To reiterate the important points of this story, God said, "You did not believe me!" What Moses did not believe was God's goodness. He didn't believe in God's gracious and forgiving character. He couldn't believe God would simply give the people water without some punishment also. So one important aspect of believing in God is to believe in his goodness, his graciousness. The sin of unbelief is to reject God's goodness, and in this case it was manifested by rash words.

This same perspective on the deeper attitude of unbelief is seen in the New Testament when Jesus disputed with the religious leaders of his day. His problem with them was their unbelief (John 3:18; 4:48; 5:38; 8:24). He was constantly focusing on the issue of faith as the way to God's salvation. Belief or unbelief also gave any deed its moral color. He said in John 5:38, "You do not have God's word abiding in you because you do not believe in him whom he has sent." He was saying this to people who knew God's word backward and forward. Jesus was telling them, "You don't know anything. I can tell by your unbelief."

If you study the gospel of Matthew, you will find that Jesus uses the term "hypocrisy" to describe a heart of unbelief. Quoting Isaiah,

Jesus said, "You hypocrites! Isaiah was right when he prophesied about you: 'These people honor me with their lips, but their hearts are far from me'" (Matt. 15:7–8). What is a hypocrite? Someone whose heart is far from God (unbelief) and whose actions may even be quite religious! Jesus was saying there is something deeper than deeds—the heart attitude. Because these people did not have a heart of faith towards God, whatever they said or did was hypocritical. It was all sinful. They were faking loyalty to God when their hearts were in a state of unbelief.

Paul is straightforward in his description of sin. In Romans 14:23 he says, ". . . everything that does not come from faith is sin." Even a decision that *seems* good from the outside is sinful if it is not done in an attitude of faith.

What is faith?

The question that naturally flows from this discussion is, "What is faith?" If sinning is unbelief, then what does it mean to believe?

Hebrews 11:6 defines faith by saying:

> And without faith it is impossible to please God, because anyone who comes to him must believe that he exists and that he rewards those who earnestly seek him.

First, one who has faith in God must believe in his existence. That much is obvious. God has made his presence in this world known. He has left behind much evidence, and he continues to reveal himself through the Scriptures. Yet he has also been subtle enough that choosing God requires *as much faith* as choosing other options.

However, believing that God exists is not enough for biblically-sound faith. Have you ever had a friend who said, "Yeah, I believe in God," but you sensed something was not right? James points out that even God's enemy, Satan, believes God is there (James 2:19).

Hebrews 11:6 says we also must believe he is a loving God—He loves me. We have to come to the point where we believe he will reward us if we seek Him. This was the situation with Moses. To believe in God is to believe in His love and goodness. This is why faith is active. Real faith motivates us to choose, to seek, to want God's way because we believe he will give us the best. I could understand someone who says, "I'm not sure that God's ways are best. I think I need to check around first." Obviously that person would not seek God because he suffers from a lack of faith.

On the other hand, what if someone said, "I believe God has the best thing. I believe he would reward me if I sought him out, but I just don't want to." What could this mean? Most likely, it means he doesn't really believe God is loving. People who say they believe that God has the best for them but don't seek him out usually have some hidden doubts. The truth is they believe God will take something away from them if they submit to him. They think he will give them something less than what they could get for themselves. So they pretend. They don't want to boldly say, "I think God is a rip-off!" but their actions reveal what they really believe.

Summary

God is loving. This conviction lies at the heart of faith and is what persuades us to turn our lives over to him and trust him. Sin, on the other hand, is the natural tendency to resist God, which is at the heart of unbelief. A heart of unbelief says, "I'll live my life independently. I'll do my own thing." If I have a heart of unbelief I can't throw myself at God because I *do not believe* in his love. I do not believe he will provide for me. I do not believe his ways are the best. I may have this attitude when I do something blatantly contrary to God's will or I could be doing something that appears to be good. It's a matter of whether I am giving myself over to God and depending on him or trusting in my own abilities.

The Bible teaches that sin is a violation of God's standards, but this is not the whole picture. Sin is more than a violation of the rules. Sin is a heart of unbelief no matter how it is manifested. Sin can be seen in the godless drug dealer who believes he can get more from what he is doing than from following God. But as Jesus' interaction with the religious leaders of his day demonstrates, sin is also seen in the well-behaved religious persons who are living with an attitude of self-reliance rather than faith.

It is amazing to see how many ways unbelief can manifest itself! If a person trusts in himself more than in God, he may still live a life that appears quite religious. It makes him feel good about himself. Or maybe he gets money and power from a religious facade. Whatever the reasons, the Bible is clear that the final word on an action will not be based on the way it appeared, but on "the motives of men's hearts" (1 Cor. 4:5).

Application

When we understand God's view of sin, we also see some powerful implications. Let's consider these implications as we apply the biblical doctrine of sin to our lives.

It's easy to trivialize sin.

If people saw sin for what it is and really believed it, there would be a lot more serious Christians. Some Christians are extremely legalistic—making a big deal out of the slightest infraction of some arbitrary standard. Other Christians seem to take liberty to do whatever they want and then sing songs about their love for God.

The problem with both extremes is that they trivialize sin.

The legalist defines sin and holiness in terms of an external code—which, by the way, is usually easy to keep. He will select certain portions of God's standards and hold them up as the goal of holiness, because, truly, if we were open to the whole of God's standards, we would be exposed for who we really are.

I remember at one stage in my life being obsessed with how many people I shared the gospel with. In fact, I would quantify my own spiritual health by noting I had successfully shared Christ with someone recently. "If people are coming to Christ around me, I must be doing things right." Even when I obviously hurt people with my actions or my tongue, I could claim I was still living for God although my pride was so swollen it was like a sign on my forehead. I could ignore the conviction of the Spirit because I was keeping a standard.

I didn't take my standard directly from the Ten Commandments. But the legalist looks at a standard (usually a biblical standard, mind you) and says, "This is what it is to perform God's will." And that is why a legalist can be so hard on people. His conscience is satisfied by keeping a standard. He is able to criticize others with a great deal of self-confident back-patting. His conscience tells him nothing is wrong.

When I was in college, I once became upset with an older Christian for buying what I considered to be an extravagant luxury. I was vocal about it. I had no problem pointing out to others that this supposedly mature Christian felt pretty free and easy with God's money. Then it came to my attention that I rarely ever gave money to the Lord's work. "But I'm too poor," I would complain. "I'm having a hard time keeping my own head above water." But I did have enough money for plenty of pizzas, movies, and the fun times that college students usually have.

The older Christian may have been guilty of careless spending or even over-indulgence. I, on the other hand, was self-centered with my money. I was not generous. On top of it all, I was extremely judgmental.

This is how legalists look at sin: as a violation of a few standards. They consider the most serious standards to be those they no longer violate. Worse yet, they can satisfy their own consciences by saying, "Look, I do the right things and I refrain from the wrong things! I must be doing okay." There is little motivation for real spiritual growth with that kind of attitude.

If we understood sin for what it is—unbelief, a lack of dependence on God—then we would be humbled. We would be hungry for God. I have to realize that I could check off my list of good deeds each day and still have a heart of unbelief. I could avoid all the bad things and still be entirely sinful because sin has to do with the heart attitude.

I once taught a Bible study where I wasn't very concerned with how things turned out. I had no real desire to depend on God for that study. I was just doing my job. I would prepare something from the Bible and go teach it. But there was no drive to pray, seek out the Lord's guidance, or draw on his strength. Some may consider the teaching of God's word a "good work." Not necessarily. In this case, what I did may have been *better* than doing nothing. Yet God's will is that I seek him out, believe in him, and depend on him to work through me.

At the other legalistic extreme, there are people who have little regard for God's will, even as Christians. They have a relaxed attitude towards sin. This type of person is called "licentious" because he or she takes God's grace as a license for his own continued sinfulness. Their attitude is, "If I can get away with it, it must not be that serious." Again, this person is not understanding the real problem, a heart of unbelief toward God.

A person who wallows in failure with sin in their life is either: a) underestimating how serious the problem is (and therefore not taking it very seriously) or b) unbelieving about how great God's salvation can be. Our discussion of sin is aimed at the first problem. Of course, it takes time and experience to see the truth about the depth of our sins. There is no way around that. When a licentious person says, "Oh well, I messed up again," they are looking at their sins as individual, isolated events. They are thinking, "Maybe I'll do better next time."

The shocking truth is that individual sins in our lives are a sign of alienation from God. I'm not talking about alienation in the sense of God being angry at us. The Bible teaches that from God's side there is only perfect love and acceptance toward believers. Even if we continue to struggle with sin, God's love doesn't waver (Rom. 8:38–39). However, the same is not true for us. On a personal level, we can grow distant from the God who loves us. We may enter into a state that dilutes our *experience* of God's love.

The image Jesus used to describe this was of a son and a father (Luke 15:11–32). The son decided to run off and enjoy his own experience, which turned into a nightmare of loss and consequences. Eventually the son decided to return, only to find the father eagerly awaiting. The son felt shameful and unworthy, but the father excitedly embraced his son and wept. This is God's love for us. Yet, sometimes we go our own way and have a hard time experiencing that love.

Hebrews warns readers about this possibility in chapters 3 and 4. They warn us that we may fail to enter into God's rest—a metaphor for a happy and productive Christian life. Hebrews 3:13 cautions against one particular hazard:

> But encourage one another daily, as long as it is called Today, so that none of you may be hardened by sin's deceitfulness.

We need to watch out for the possibility of hardening our hearts by continued sinfulness. In the Bible, hardening refers to a stubbornness, a state of mind that resists God. Hebrews warns us that by sinfulness we can slip into a stubborn state of mind that will deprive us of the full experience of God in this life.

Can you could imagine being married to someone who constantly goes out and has affairs? Stretch your imagination further and picture yourself always welcoming your spouse back, always having a heart of unwavering love towards him or her! Then you would be getting close to the way God's love is for us and the way we often take it for granted. There is no doubt, however, that the adulterous spouse would experience very few of the joys of marriage.

If only the licentious person would see the issue is not *this* sin or *that* sin. The point is not to try to gauge whether we can afford to stumble. The point is, do I want a close relationship with God or not? Do I realize my sins can be a sign of hostility between myself and the God who gave His life for me? (James 4:4). Obviously the hostility does not come from God toward us. Yet God is very clear that to reject him and his ways is to be hostile toward him. If we desire to be close to him, we will do what he wants (Rom. 8:4).

When I was first trying to come to terms with my own casual attitude toward sin, I was a young Christian struggling with substance abuse. There weren't many substances I didn't abuse. The main question for me was, "Will it help me feel better?" Of course I knew my actions were sinful, but what I didn't understand was how serious the sin was. I kept thinking, "Oh no, I blew it again! Next time I'll have to be stronger." The real truth was that I was far from God. God and I were virtual strangers even though His Spirit lived within me.

As I saw the distance between God and myself, I began to long for a closer relationship. I heard from people about his love, but I never saw it or experienced it in my life. I began to wonder, "Is it possible to be close to God? Can I have what other Christians have?" I recall a time of prayer at a weekend retreat where many people were praising God for how good he was, how loving he was, how thankful they were for His involvement in their lives. I piped up with my confused and tortured prayer, "God, I have no idea what these people are talking about." That was it. I couldn't voice anything more. Yet that was the beginning of my victory over repeated failure. I began to see that the issue was my completely hollow relationship with God. Trying to avoid this sin or that sin was insufficient. I had to go deeper and try to resolve the alienation between God and myself. Practically speaking, this meant that I began to pray in earnest, immersing myself in Christian fellowship, and developing a hunger for God's Word. These positive pursuits quickly eliminated my feeble crutches.

We need to look at root causes.

Our understanding of sin as unbelief will also affect how we deal with people. If we view sin as a mere violation of rules, then we might scold people for infractions, "Stop that! Don't you know that's a sin!?" This is the sum total of the help many Christians offer one another.

On the other hand, if we understand the deeper attitude behind sin, we would see that particular violations are merely symptoms of a deeper problem. It's no use attacking the symptom if we don't also address the deeper issue.

I participated in a Sunday school program that didn't allow us to snipe at each other. Since only kind words were tolerated, we didn't say much. What's worse, when friends were upset with each other, they would just part ways. Instead of dealing with the problem, the external focus forced it to come out in different ways—ways that were more damaging than sniping words.

The deeper issue in negative relationships with people is faith in God—faith that godly love is truly the best; faith that he can transform our selfishness; faith that he can help us forgive. Real love doesn't mean simply the absence of sniping. Real love will come when we decide to trust God and follow his ways in our relationships.

As we work with people and deal with our own sin problems, we need to realize particular acts of disobedience are merely manifestations of deeper attitudes. We should take the time to listen, understand why someone is struggling, draw out their deeper attitudes, and let them come to terms with God in a more personal way. The net result will be a more positive approach to working with people. We realize that they are not going to stop their sins today, tomorrow, or even the next day. The particular sin will stop gradually as God deals with the long-term attitudes. In the meantime, we have to decide if we can accept, forgive, and love someone who sins. The question is, Can I love that person just as he or she is?

Conclusion

We have been looking at the nature of sin. We see it is far more than the violation of a standard. Sin is an attitude of independence—a lack of faith. Sin is obvious when we're breaking rules, but it is just as present when we are doing "good things" with a heart of unbelief.

There are some important practical applications of the doctrine of sin. If we truly understand sin, we won't trivialize it by making it "merely" a violation of God's law. This is the mistake of both legalists and licentious people. The former try to measure their lives by a standard and hopefully appease their conscience by complying with the letter of the law. The licentious people also don't understand the seriousness of sin. If they did, they wouldn't feel like they could "get away with it." They would see sin as a sign of their strained relationship with God.

But where did sin come from? How were we born with such a serious problem? Is it really fair that we have this inherent weakness? These are the questions we need to look at next.

Study summary

We started with the topic of sin because it is the central issue between God and us. Here are some of the key concepts and Scriptures we covered in this chapter:

Key Points
- Sin is more than the violation of a standard; it is unbelief (Rom. 14:23).
- Faith is more than believing that God exists. It also means to believe in God's goodness and love. If we really do believe in God's love, we will seek him out (Heb. 11:6).
- It is easy to trivialize sin, dismissing it as only a physical habit

or occasional lapse. The truth is, sin is tied to the very essence of our nature as prideful, independent creatures.
- One way to trivialize sin is by focusing on a selection of external, legalistic rules. Others are licentious, taking God's grace for granted because they fail to recognize the seriousness of sin.

Key Scriptures
- Romans 5:12
- Hebrews 11:6
- Romans 14:23

Important Terms
- Sin
  Falling short of a standard. This is the most common use of the term in our everyday speech. "I sinned today; I lied."

  A tendency toward sin within us. The Bible sometimes uses the term to refer to a propensity toward sinfulness that characterizes the entire human race. "We all have sin because we inherited it from Adam."

  Unbelief. Deeper than the violation of a standard and more than any particular act, sin is unbelief.

- Faith / Belief
  Entrusting yourself to the goodness and love of God. Biblical faith is more than believing God exists; it means to believe God is loving. If we believe that God is loving, we will trust what he says and entrust our lives to him. That is why faith always implies action.

For Further Reading
- *Sin and Temptation* by John Owen, Multnomah Press, 1983
- *Offense to Reason: A Theology of Sin* by Bernard Ramm, Harper and Row, 1985

CHAPTER TWO

UNDERSTANDING HUMANS

The first people

Even people who don't know much about the Bible know Adam and Eve ate the forbidden fruit.

But the first chapters of Genesis are telling us much more than the simple fact that two people disobeyed God. Genesis explains the discord between humans and God. It is teaching us what sin is all about.

The forbidden tree in the garden was called "the tree of the knowledge of good and evil." That is a long name so many people often shorten it to "the tree of good and evil." But they are missing a crucial point that Genesis is making. Doing good or evil was not the issue that day. The issue was the *knowledge* of good and evil. On the day Adam and Eve ate the fruit, the human race tapped into a new source of knowledge about good and evil.

Think of it this way. Before Adam and Eve ate the fruit, how did they know what was good or evil? God told them. God was their source of morality and direction. This was a relationship between people and their Creator that Genesis describes as "walking together" (Gen. 3:8). In other words, Adam and Eve were intimately and personally taking their cue from their Creator. Then an opportunity came along and they imagined, "I could decide for myself what is good or bad!" The Bible phrases it that the fruit, "made one wise, like God, knowing the difference between good and evil" (Gen. 3:5–6).

Both Adam and Eve chose to take on the responsibility of deciding the standards of morality for themselves. It was not free will they gained; obviously the decision they made showed they already had that capacity. What they gained was the ability to make up their own standard of right and wrong.

Immediately, Adam and Even thought it was wrong to be naked. The Bible tells us they saw they were naked, and they were ashamed (Gen. 3:7). This is a great picture of what Adam and Eve gained and what they lost. They gained an ability to have their conscience accuse them and make them feel guilty. They lost the freedom to be comfortable with each other and even with God. When God came to spend time with them, they ran and hid in shame. Although Adam and Eve didn't need anyone to tell them about right and wrong anymore, this new capacity bound them up and restricted them more than they ever could have imagined.

Ever since that time, humans have decided things for themselves. We run our own lives without depending on God. At the same time, we bear the guilt, anxiety, and pressure that come from being independent. God's original design included freedom of choice and responsibility. Adam and Eve were so free, in fact, that there was only one thing they could not do—eat of the tree of the knowledge of good and evil. God's plan also included a close, dependent relationship with him in which we look to him for guidance and strength. The notion of freedom and dependence are not mutually exclusive.

As we consider the study of humans, we will look at what God originally meant for us to be and what we have become instead.

The original picture

God created Adam and Eve perfect in a perfect world. God called it "good" and "very good" (Gen. 1:31). The term "perfect" conveys completeness and the idea that nothing more can be added. But actually, God created a world designed for improvement. He fully intended for Adam and Eve to make things better, as he commanded them to "cultivate and keep" the world he had made (Gen. 2:15).

But what was it about Adam and Eve that was "good"? We can see several things from these opening chapters of Genesis.

Spiritual beings

First, Adam and Eve were created as spiritual beings. They were different from any other part of creation because they were like God— spiritual. Genesis says of each type of plant and animal, God created them "after their kind" (see Gen. 1:11, 21, 24–25). Not so with humans. We were created "after the image of God" (Gen. 1:26). This is the contrast Genesis establishes in the first chapter. Every other created thing is "after their kind," meaning that they have a basic

affiliation. Mankind is different from all the others, being more like
God in his spiritual and eternal life.

This truth is put another way in Genesis 2:7, where God breathed
the breath of life into Adam. As a result, "Adam became a living
soul." God gave Adam a spiritual dimension unlike any other created
being. Elsewhere the Bible interprets the "breath of God" to be God's
Spirit (see Job 33:4; 34:14).

The spiritual side of our humanity is something we understand so
little about. Most of our learning and knowledge is limited to the
physical side of life. That is the only way we perceive. That is the
only way we experiment. That is how we remember. So where is our
spiritual dimension?

It could be that when Adam and Even sinned, their spiritual capacity
was crippled. God warned Adam and Eve that the very day they ate
of the tree, they would "surely die" (Genesis 2:17). This death was
obviously not physical; it was a spiritual death. Sin destroyed Adam
and Eve's spiritual nature. We'll look into this more when we discuss
what has happened since the Fall.

Productive

Second, we learn that God intended humans to be productive and
useful. He gave Adam and Eve a command "to cultivate and keep"
the world they lived in (Gen. 2:15). This meant they were to develop
it, nurture it, and make it better. This is the first example of human
work in the Bible and it is a great example of what work was meant
to be. Adam and Eve had "good" resources and their task was to
make them *better*. What an ideal work setting—a setting where
everything you do is productive, all the resources are good, and you
have the freedom to be as creative as you please!

Able to choose

In Genesis 2:17, God warns Adam and Eve not to eat from the tree
of the knowledge of good and evil. He gave them the awesome power
of choice—something we value quite a bit today. Choice is the
cornerstone of another favorite word: freedom.

However, the notion of "free choice" is misleading. It gives the
impression that somehow our choices are not hindered. In fact, no
one has absolute free choice. I could not become an egg or Captain
Kangaroo. When we look closely, there are probably more limitations
on our choices than there are freedoms.

What, then, is free choice? In the context of our relationship with
God, it is the ability to choose for or against him. That is the power

Adam and Eve had. They were given one opportunity to choose against their Creator. If a relationship means anything, there must be this option. People who love each other must have the choice not to love. Otherwise, we would talk about good old friends the same way we would talk about good old boots or a good old car. I have a fondness for my possessions but they have no choice but to be faithful to me. If I really choose to love someone, it should be because I can also choose not to love them.

I raise this issue because some people wonder why God put the temptation of the tree in the garden with Adam and Eve. Why not let them live in a world without temptation? In that situation there would be no choice but to have a relationship with God, which means the relationship would be meaningless.

Relational

The fourth characteristic of humans before the Fall is that they were relational. All through the creation account, God was saying, "This is good. This is good. This is very good . . ." Then, one thing caused him to say, "This is not good!" Adam was alone (Gen. 2:18). This statement jumps out, "Something is not right here!" God solved the problem by creating the perfect counterpart: woman. The creation of woman added an exciting dimension to the relational side of humanity—sexuality. But the reason Adam was lonely was because he was created to have relationships.

Genesis seems to portray God as surprised at Adam's loneliness. He has Adam review all the animals to make sure none of them could be a good friend. Then, as a last resort, God creates Eve. The real point of the story, however, is to accentuate just how much we were designed to have relationships with other people. Adam was in a perfect world. He had opportunity for accomplishment, creativity, and relaxation. He was in perfect harmony with the entire creation, as shown by his interaction with every other animal. But things were still not right! It was "not good," according to God. Adam's dilemma teaches us that we could have every other thing in the world but if we don't have closeness with other humans, it's just no good.

Rather than being an afterthought, Eve was an important part of God's plan. The story demonstrates that he created us for one another. The ultimate relationship on earth is between a male and female when they get married. Genesis describes this relationship at the end of chapter 2, "For this cause a man shall leave his father and his mother, and shall cleave to his wife; and they shall become one flesh." The goal is absolute unity—oneness. I don't want to minimize the possibility of deep and satisfying love for single people. I truly believe that a Christian could remain single and grow to have very godly, loving relationships. In fact, the most highly regarded chapter on love in the entire Bible was written by Paul the apostle, who was single (see 1 Cor. 13).

Genesis concludes the creation story on a striking note: "And the man and his wife were both naked and were not ashamed" (v. 25). "They were not ashamed," portends trouble. Why bring up the notion of shame here? It also describes an amazing degree of openness. Here is a picture of the depth God intends for relationships. He wants us to have relationships so close and open that we have nothing to be ashamed of. It's hard to grasp this degree of closeness. Have you ever met anyone who had nothing to hide?

Now that we've seen what humans were meant to be, we'll look at how our nature has been warped by sin.

After the fall

Adam and Eve chose to go their own way, as we discussed above. What happened? What is the human state we have inherited?

Death

First of all, God promised that one of the results of eating of the tree would be Adam and Eve's death. Death is a concept Adam and Eve weren't familiar with. What did they have to compare it to? They had never seen anyone or anything die.

What they did know was life. There are several biblical pictures which describe life. In the early chapters of Genesis and throughout the Bible, life is from God. Life is a relationship with God, being intimate with God. If you will recall, the "breath of life" came directly from God into Adam. There was also a "tree of life" in the garden next to the tree of the knowledge of good and evil. In the book of Revelation, John understands the tree of life to be synonymous with a relationship with God (Rev. 22:14). The imagery is similar to Jesus' repeated offers of "life" (John 10:10) or the "bread of life" (John 6:35, 48) or "living water" (John 7:38). All these metaphors are descriptions of getting right with God and coming back into a relationship with him.

So Adam knew life was from God. Clearly, death is separation from God. Adam knew as he chose to rebel and eat of the fruit, his entire relationship with God hung in the balance.

Today we have examples of death all around us. We see animals and plants die. We see ourselves slowly dying. Our tendency is to look at death purely in terms of the termination of our physical bodies. In reality, though, our physical death is just a symptom of the real death—separation from God. It is because we *are* dead that we are decaying. God intended to sustain us and supply us with his life forever. When that source was cut off, the machine we live in started to wind down and eventually quit.

Death is separation from God. Adam chose death. But the sad state of humanity is that each one of us chooses death every day. We want to be independent from God. We want to run our own lives. We want to be our own gods. This independence from God is the source of all the death at work around us.

Earlier we talked about the spiritual dimension of humans. We are often puzzled by our spiritual side. It seems we only realize this crucial aspect of our humanity when we are restored to a relationship with God. The alienation from him, described by the term "death," also repressed our spiritual endowment. The Bible makes this clear when it talks about conversion as being "made alive" spiritually. Paul describes this transition in Ephesians 2:5:

> [God] made us alive with Christ even when we were dead in transgressions—it is by grace you have been saved.

Once we are made alive, we grow spiritually. Our spiritual side becomes more noticeable and powerful. Some New Testament references to this process include: Colossians 3:9–10; Ephesians 4:22–24; Galatians 5:16–24.

So then, the state we inherit from Adam and Eve is spiritual dormancy—spiritual death. It is a state where we are out of touch with God. As a result, we are out of touch with our spiritual heritage because he is the one who brings our spiritual side to life. Therefore, non-Christians sense something is missing. Intuitively they know there is an entire realm of their human character that is lifeless. This is why people go hunting for spiritual experiences or numb themselves with over-indulgence in work, chemicals, or other pleasures to temporarily fill the emptiness.

Relational alienation

As well as alienation from God, Adam and Eve began to experience something we are all too familiar with—alienation from one another. Relational alienation is a fact of life for us but it must have come as a rude shock to Adam and Eve. One minute they were standing there, naked and unashamed. The next minute they were blushing with embarrassment running to find some leaves to cover up! The account tells us they sewed fig leaves together to make a covering. Fig leaves are small—about the size of oak leaves. Their attempt at a cover-up—both physical and spiritual—would have been humorous if it had not been so tragic.

This was just the beginning of the distance that would characterize human relationships all through history. When God came to talk to Adam and Eve about what happened, they began to blame each other. Adam said, "The woman you put here with me—she gave me some fruit from the tree, and I ate it" (Gen. 3:12). As God explained to them what would happen as a result of their choice, he said something truly ominous to Eve, "Your desire will be for your husband, but he will rule over you" (Gen. 3:16). God was thinking how bad things were going to get in human history. Women would desire to have a relationship with men but instead men would rule over and subdue women. One of the most angering themes of human history is the male mistreatment of females. Men have taken a relationship that was meant to be so close, "the two should become one," and turned it into an ordeal of domination.

Sadly, some Christians have taken these words of God in Genesis 3:16 to describe how things ought to be. Usually they are men who state, "You ought to desire me and I am supposed to rule over you." Nothing could be further from the truth! The context of this statement is God describing the sad and fallen state Adam and Eve had chosen. God also dictated that there would be pain in childbirth (v. 16) and man would contend with thorns and thistles (v. 18). That is why the pronouncements of Genesis 3:14–19 are sometimes called "The Curse." I don't like that term because it insinuates that the bad things that ensued were all God's doing. Instead, it was humans who chose to be alienated from God. God simply described to Adam and Eve the new course they had chosen. It would be a course where humans would be their own gods. An individual's own ego would reign supreme. And man as the physically stronger being would rule, dominate, and conquer anything and anyone he could.

This alienation can be seen full-blown in the children of Adam and Eve. The first murder occurred when their oldest son, Cain, killed his brother out of jealousy. Several generations later a man named Lamech, who took two wives, perfectly embodied the dreadful choice Adam and Eve made:

> Lamech said to his wives, "Adah and Zillah, listen to me; wives of Lamech, hear my words. I have killed a man for wounding me, a young man for injuring me" (Gen. 4:23).

So it goes. We have been more concerned with how to protect ourselves from each other than how to get close and make ourselves vulnerable and open to each other—exactly the opposite of God's original plan. What other course is there when each person wants to be their own god? Doesn't it come down to who can control whom? Who has the most power? Who can get his or her way?

This is the sad state of human relationships apart from God.

Alienation from the world

The third result of the Fall was that humans were at odds with the world around them. Previously, God had placed humans at the top of the chain of life. "You are to control the earth and rule over it," God told them (Gen. 1:28). However, their authority was supposed to be loving for the good of the earth. As God told them later, "Take care of it" (Gen. 2:15).

· After their choice, God warned Adam and Eve that the earth would become their adversary.

> Cursed is the ground because of you; through painful toil you will eat of it all the days of your life. It will produce thorns and thistles for you, and you will eat the plants of the field. By the sweat of your brow you will eat your food until you return to the ground, since from it you were taken; for dust you are and to dust you will return (Gen. 3:17–19).

God would no longer maintain the cooperative relationship between humans and their environment. He turned them loose to struggle with each other. In essence he was saying, "If you want to be your own god, then you'll have to figure out how to subdue some mighty powerful forces I've put here on the earth." Ever since then, humans have faced a prolonged struggle of trying to rule a world that isn't very cooperative. Constant mutations, diseases, and destructive forces make it hard to be our own gods and subdue the earth.

Ultimately each human is defeated as our physical bodies deteriorate and give way to death.

Choice restricted

Finally, Adam and Eve's decision to rebel against God, ironically, severely restricted their freedom of choice. Before the Fall, they could choose to fellowship with God and obey him. They could also choose to reject him. After the Fall, however, they lost their choice to fellowship with God in the way they had before. It's put this way in Genesis 3:24:

> After he drove the man out, he placed on the east side of the Garden of Eden cherubim and a flaming sword flashing back and forth to guard the way to the tree of life.

The "tree of life" signified fellowship with God and His life. Now that Adam and Eve had chosen the way of independence, they couldn't turn back and have the same intimacy they once enjoyed with God.

The ultimate tragedy is that humans may feel the freedom to be their own gods but they are *not free* to fellowship and relate to the real God. It is only by God's mercy that he has come to rescue us from this one-way street.

Conclusion

We have been discussing the fruit of our independence. Humans have chosen to take matters into their own hands. In the process, we have rejected the authority of our Creator. We have grown alienated from one another and pour countless energies into surviving and coping in this world.

It would be a mistake to think Adam and Eve's choice was theirs and not ours. Some people read of Adam and Eve and think, "But I would have chosen differently! It's not fair!"

For one thing, it should be obvious to each of us that we don't choose differently. Each minute of each day we choose to live our own lives, be our own authorities, and decide what is right and wrong for ourselves. We choose to be our own gods. It is the epitome of our own blindness to think we would have chosen differently.

Everywhere we look the choices of one person affect another. This is a basic truth of human existence. It is the very nature of a family. It is the choice of a parent to have a child. The parent's actions will affect that child for the rest of his or her life. That is how God designed human beings. He did not make each person alone like an island. He made the first two who had the awesome responsibility of affecting the rest of humanity.

If you are extremely bothered with the unfairness of this economy, I would suggest you avoid hypocrisy by isolating yourself from all human contact. By choosing to drive a car, you could kill an entire family. Your choice would snuff out the lives of other living persons together with all the children they might have had! If you have children, everything about you affects those children. If you work, your attitudes and choices have an effect on all your fellow employees. Ironically, even choosing to remove yourself from this cause and effect world would have a profound impact on others! Imagine the people you might have affected! Imagine the children you might have had! Imagine the good (or bad) you might have done!

It would be strange to live in a world where nobody influenced anyone else. In fact, there is a brilliance to the system God has created, especially when we understand he intended that influence to be positive.

Now we can turn to what God has done to remedy this tragic situation.

Study summary

Key Points

- Before choosing to sin, humans were created by God to be free, to have meaningful responsibility, to be relational, and to have a close relationship with God.
- After the Fall (Adam and Eve's choice to sin), all these qualities were either severely warped or lost altogether.
- The choice to sin was a choice to be independent from God as the name of "the tree of the knowledge of good and evil," indicates. Before the Fall, God was the one to define good and evil. Afterwards, Adam and Eve were able to do it themselves but along with this new ability they suffered alienation from God.

Key Scriptures

- Genesis 2 and 3

Important Terms

- Image of God
  To be more like God than any other created thing. God said he created us in his image which means to be spiritual, like God, and to be able to relate to him.

- Free will
  To be able to obey or refuse God's will in some areas. Free will does not mean the freedom to do anything I want. Nor does it mean to have the freedom to reject all of God's will. Free will, in the context of our relationship with God, means to be able refuse his gracious overtures towards us.

- Death
  Separation from God. There can be varying stages of death. Spiritual separation from God results in physical deterioration

because he is no longer sustaining us the way he did before. Ultimately, hell will be complete separation from God.

For Further Reading

- *The Pentateuch as Narrative* by John Sailhammer, Zondervan, 1992
- *Genesis in Space and Time* by Francis Schaeffer, InterVarsity Press, 1972
- *Understanding Man* by Ray Stedman, Multnomah, 1975
- *Knowing Man* by J. I. Packer , Crossway Books, 1978
- *Created in God's Image* by Anthony Hoekema, Wm. B. Eerdmans, 1986

CHAPTER THREE

GOD HAD A PLAN

As soon as Adam and Eve made the choice to reject God's authority, God had a plan to fix things. He hinted at his plan when he addressed the group of conspirators, Adam, Eve, and the Serpent. To Satan he said, "I will put enmity between you and the woman, and between your offspring and hers; he will crush your head, and you will strike his heel" (Gen. 3:15).

The first part of the prediction said Eve and Satan would be at odds. It's not hard to understand why. God also said a particular descendant would come who would conflict with Satan. God predicted the outcome would be the undoing of Satan—a "crushed head," so to speak. In the process, Satan would also hurt Eve's offspring.

Eve may have thought God was referring to one of her immediate children. Far from it! God's plan, as usual, was bigger than anyone could have imagined. As successive generations sought to follow God, he gradually revealed his intentions to save the human race. First he picked out one family—the family of Abraham in Genesis 12. God told Abraham he wanted to use him and his family to undo the terrible mess humans had made. He put it this way to Abraham:

> I will make you into a great nation and I will bless you; I will make your name great, and you will be a blessing. I will bless those who bless you, and whoever curses you I will curse; and all peoples on earth will be blessed through you (Genesis 12:2–3).

God promised Abraham that he would be the source of blessing for the whole world. Blessing is not a common term today. But in this passage it has so much power we don't want to overlook it.

The entire Bible up to this point had been one long story of *cursings* or disasters which befell the human race. There was the curse of Adam and Eve. Not long after that, the entire human race grew so corrupt that God judged the world, saving only Noah and his family. Once again, it wasn't long before humans were plotting how they might overthrow God's authority under the leadership of a great king named Nimrod at the first city of Babylon. God moved in judgment again— this time separating humans by confusing their languages. One epoch after another ended in disaster for humans.

Now God told Abraham, "I want to bless people through you." God wanted to undo the damage.

Abraham became the father of the nation of Israel. God promised the Israelites that through them he would send a deliverer for the whole world. But this Savior would not be just any Israelite. God narrowed his promise to the household of Israel's greatest king—King David. He promised David that one of his descendants would bring salvation to the whole world. Through the prophet Nathan, God said:

> And it shall come about when your days are fulfilled that you must go to be with your fathers, that I will set up one of your descendants after you, who shall be of your sons; and I will establish his kingdom. He shall build for Me a house, and I will establish his throne forever. I will be his father, and he shall be My son; and I will not take My lovingkindness away from him, as I took it from him who was before you. But I will settle him in My house and in My kingdom forever, and his throne shall be established forever (1 Chron. 17:11–14).

The coming deliverer was also to be a king! In other passages, God made it clear that his kingdom would be worldwide (see Amos 9:11–12). As the Old Testament prophets spoke of this long-awaited Savior, they made some startling predictions. Isaiah predicted in Isaiah 9:1–2 that this deliverer would be "light to the Gentiles of Galilee (the hill country in northern Israel, which is where Jesus spent most of his life)." But he went on and said:

> For to us a child is born, to us a son is given, and the government will be on his shoulders. And he will be called Wonderful Counselor, Mighty God, Everlasting Father, Prince of Peace. Of the increase of his government and peace there will be no end. He will reign on David's throne and over his kingdom, establishing and upholding it with justice and righteousness from that time on and forever. The zeal of the Lord Almighty will accomplish this (Isaiah 9:6–7).

It makes sense to call this ruler a "Wonderful Counselor." Rulers are supposed to be wise. But Isaiah also calls him, "Mighty God!" What is this? "Everlasting Father!?"

This is the first place in the Bible where it becomes clear that the coming Savior was not just a great man. He would be God in the flesh. God was going to embody himself in a human frame and become the deliverer he had promised so long ago to Adam and Eve!

God enters history

About 600 years after Isaiah, the angel Gabriel approached a woman named Mary. Gabriel's message was unusual,

> You will be with child and give birth to a son, and you are to give him the name Jesus. He will be great and will be called the Son of the Most High. The Lord God will give him the throne of his father David, and he will reign over the house of Jacob forever; his kingdom will never end (Luke 1:31–33).

Gabriel explained to Mary that this son would be born miraculously, as she was still a virgin. God himself would be the one to place a child within her. Everything the entire world waited for, everything the Old Testament pointed to, was about to happen through this young girl!

Understandably she was disturbed by this announcement. Mary began to pray for strength from the Lord to deal with such a calling. Most people know how God affirmed Mary and her new husband, Joseph, in many ways by sending "wise men" from another country along with other visitors (read Luke 2:1–38).

Who was Jesus Christ?

Jesus was God in the form of a human. This union of divine and human natures has always puzzled those who read the Bible. A pair of biblical passages give us more insight.

Colossians 2:9
Paul put it very simply:

> For in Christ all the fullness of the Deity lives in bodily form.

From this passage we can see that in every respect Jesus was God. He embodied the "fullness" of Deity. The term "fullness" means the "full measure" or "sum total." Everything God is was embodied in Jesus Christ.

There is more. You could get the impression from Colossians 2:9 that Jesus was just God with a physical body. Jesus had more in common with us than just a physical body.

Hebrews 2:17

The writer of Hebrews tells us Jesus had much in common with us:

> For this reason he had to be made like his brothers in every way, in order that he might become a merciful and faithful high priest in service to God, and that he might make atonement for the sins of the people.

Jesus was "like his [human] brothers in every way." That's why Jesus could serve as a mediator—a priest—between ourselves and God. Jesus was the perfect mediator since he was *both* human and divine.

How can Jesus have two natures?

But how can one person have two natures? In theological terms, the union of the human and divine nature is called the "hypostatic union," a term that dates to the fifth century when Christians were hotly debating the nature of Jesus Christ. It means that the "real nature" or "essence" of Jesus Christ was both human and God. The mechanics of how one person can have two natures is something that God alone completely understands. But that doesn't mean we should view the hypostatic union as nonsense. We can still understand Jesus Christ's nature to a certain extent.

First we must understand the distinction between human nature and the person himself. Human nature is whatever it is to be human. We all share such a human nature. Yet within each human is a unique person. I am an individual who shares a common nature with all other humans.

These are not psychological definitions we can validate with a test or find in an operating room. Nevertheless, it makes sense to distinguish between universal human nature and the distinct person inside. Human nature includes things like the ability and desire to communicate, love, hate, share, cry, or laugh. It includes our limitations and aspirations and even our curiosity about God and his universe.

God also has a nature. God's nature is comprised in part of his infinity, omniscience, perfect love, and sinless character. Jesus Christ was one person who had two natures, not two persons. Somehow God had taken on another nature by becoming human. It might be something like the transition we will go through when we are transformed in the next life.

Conclusion

The prideful humans rejected God but he began to plan a way of reconciliation. That plan culminated in the birth of a Savior, Jesus Christ, who was both human and divine. It is important to understand who Jesus Christ was because his nature has such an effect on what he came to do. Jesus didn't come just to be a ruler. He didn't come just to tell us what God is like. His mission was the greatest surprise of all history. We'll turn to that issue next.

Study summary

Key Points
- After the Fall, God immediately began implementing a way of salvation. He promised to use Abraham and the nation of Israel to bring a Savior into the world.
- The Savior was going to come through the household of David, so he would be a king. But more than that, Old Testament predictions said he would be God in human form! (see Isa. 9:6).
- The New Testament clearly teaches that Jesus was both human and divine. He was God in human form (see Col. 2:9 and Heb. 2:17).

Key Scriptures
- Genesis 3:15
- Genesis 12:1–3
- 2 Chronicles 7:11–14
- Isaiah 9:6
- Colossians 2:9
- Hebrews 2:17

Important Terms
- Jesus Christ
  One person, God, who took on a second nature as a human. Jesus was both fully God and fully human. God Himself came into history as the Savior who was promised all the way through the Old Testament.

For Further Reading
- *More Than a Carpenter* by Josh McDowell, Tyndale House Publishers, 1977

- *The Mystery of the Incarnation* by Norman Anderson, InterVarsity Press, 1978
- *Jesus: A Biblical Defense of His Deity* by Josh McDowell and Bart Larson, Here's Life Publishers, 1983
- *The Person of Christ: A Biblical and Historical Analysis of the Incarnation* by David F. Wells, Crossway, 1984

CHAPTER FOUR

THE JUSTICE OF GOD

Humans need a savior

The Old Testament predicted that God would come as a Savior who would rule the world. The Jewish people anticipated this Savior as the "Messiah." But there was one serious problem: How could God rule a world that didn't want him? That was the choice Adam and Eve had made. That is the choice each one of us makes all the time—to run our own lives and reject God's authority. This is the essence of what the Bible calls "sin." How could God come and rule over people who didn't want him?

The barrier is even more pronounced. Suppose God offered to come to earth and save us from ourselves by taking charge. How would we respond? Some folks might say, "Hey, leave us alone! We like things the way they are!" But surely the majority of people would say, "OK, you can run things if you want." Of course in their minds they would think, "*Some* things, not everything!" Most people would be willing to let God take care of the world's problems but would still want the right to rule their lives their way.

From God's point of view it's not that simple. He can't just come and alleviate the world's problems. He can't just pretend like nothing is wrong. For God, there is the issue of his justice. What is he going to do about the way we treat each other? What is he going to do about all the evil things humans have invented?

If we were to give God advice, we might say, "Yes, there should be justice. Maybe you should punish some of the severe sins, maybe even judge some of the more outrageous sinners. On the other hand, most of the things I do aren't that serious. You could just let most things slide." That's how we view our own sinfulness. We think some of our sins may be "kind of" serious. But we've forgotten most of them so maybe God could too?

But God's justice is not like ours. His justice is pure. His justice is fair. His justice is absolutely just. He cannot pretend sin is not an issue. He cannot simply forget sins. We need to study God's justice, our sin, and how the Bible speaks to this dilemma.

God's justice: The problem of sliding scales

Religions all over the world have a problem with the issue of fairness, judgment, and sin. Who exactly is wicked enough to be judged by God? Should God judge anyone? If not then what about all the atrocities and evils people have committed against one another? What if God saw the child molestation and murders committed by John Gacy or Jeffrey Dahmer and did nothing about it?

It is never pleasant talking about judgment and sin. This is where people really take offense at the Christian message. Yet the more you study the issue, the better the Christian perspective looks. There are really only a few ways to address the issue of evil in this world and God's response to it.

God will judge, but only some

The first type of answer holds that God's judgment will fall on those who are extremely wicked or irreligious. Those who don't even try to be good will have to answer to God for the fact that they didn't care.

I was talking to someone about this recently. He considered himself a Christian. But when I asked him what the difference is between a Christian and a non-Christian, he was very puzzled. "Do you think God will judge anyone?" I asked. "If so, then who will he judge? How will he decide?" This guy looked really startled and said, "I've been thinking about that! I guess I don't know! I've kind of thought that he would pick people who didn't care. You know, people who were really wicked."

This is exactly where most Americans stand on the issue of God's justice. It's the kind of answer, in one form or another, many of the world religions have for the issue of God's justice. For example, Islam teaches there are certain deeds we should avoid as "sins." Such things as drinking alcohol or committing adultery are forbidden. On the other side, there are religious acts necessary to show your desire to follow God. These are the "Five Pillars of Islam." They include things like praying to God while facing Mecca, giving alms to the poor, and making a pilgrimage to Mecca at least once in your life.

Islam is typical of the religious approach to God. The religious approach seeks to appease God's justice by refraining from sin. In addition to refraining from sin, the religious approach advocates some positive religious acts and rituals that are supposed to show one's sincerity and devotion to God. Obviously no one can claim to be completely successful.

The problem with all religious approaches to God can be boiled down to one word: arbitrariness. A simpler word is "unfairness." Where should God draw the line for sins? Are there certain unforgivable sins like murder? If there is some kind of cut-off point, like a number of sins or the seriousness of sins, then what if someone is just one sin to the grief? Why draw the line at that particular point? What reason is there for allowing some sinners but not others?

The same goes for the positive religious deeds. How many religious works would someone need to do before God determined he was truly sincere? What if someone only did a few token religious observances? Where is the line between sincerity and insincerity?

Most people who believe in religious approaches to God haven't really thought about these problems. If you raise these questions, they will be at a loss for an answer. I would be very careful not to sound like a prosecutor. It may be wise to present these questions as issues you have had to wrestle with. "These were things I couldn't explain," you might say. "They really bothered me." This allows a person who holds these views to agree with you and back away from a position he hasn't thought all the way through yet.

There are some who have thought about their religious approach to God and its implications on his justice. They may reply to these objections by saying God is ultimately wise. He knows everything, including the intentions of a person's heart. Since he is completely just and knows all things, he alone is in a position to make such delicate judgments about a person's life.

If such lines are going to be drawn, there is no one who could do it better than God. Still, the distinctions he would have to make between people would be very fine indeed. It is unsatisfying to me to conceive of God making judgments between people when I know the differences are so small! Surely, for every line God could draw, there would be many, many people just one degree to either side of it! I don't care how wise God is, that kind of hair-splitting doesn't seem very fair.

Imagine standing before God and all the billions of humanity are lined up according to how sinful they were. Those to the extreme left of you were very religious and righteous. But those way down at the other end of the line were the Hitlers and Ghengis Khans of the world. Here you stand, right about in the middle. And then, God comes to the guy immediately to your left and says, "Congratulations! You're the last one to make it into heaven!" Then he casts a pitiful glance at you, "Sorry. You'll have to go now." If only you hadn't cussed that one time! If only you had controlled your lust a little better!

God won't judge anybody.
A second possible solution to the problem of justice is that God will simply forgive all people. People hold this view because they want to believe in a loving God who wouldn't judge anyone. This view fits well with the relativism that is so popular in America. Relativism is the belief that we are all talking about the same thing, even if we sound contradictory at times. Different religions are really just varying descriptions of the same God. Relativism precludes God's judgment because nobody is wrong. This answer may sound attractive at first. But it presents a serious problem:

> If God is never going to punish any wrongdoing, then why does he let things go on and on?

A God who simply forgives everything with no concern for justice removes the significance from all our decisions. What does it matter if a person chooses to live a life of savagery? What does it matter if a person tries to do good? There is no significance to the choices we make in this life. It puzzles me why God would let the current human situation go on and on when ultimately it doesn't matter what we do.

What makes this dilemma worse is that after this life, according to this scenario, we are all invited into eternal bliss. Why not just get on with it? What's the point of the suffering? What's the point of anything? If we're going to live in some kind of heaven-like state eventually, I'd just as soon do it now!

The only sensible answer is that God wants us to learn some kind of lesson here on earth. If this is true, then we have a version of hell on earth. Apparently life on this planet was meant to be a punishment or a hard lesson. This view hasn't eliminated the notion of a judging God at all. It simply changes the time and place of judgment.

This view especially angers me when I think about how suffering is different for people depending on purely arbitrary distinctions. A person's skin color or sex could land them in a world of suffering they had absolutely no say about. The people who *did* have a say— the discriminators and racists—are never brought to justice!

Suffering is also very different depending on what part of the world you come from. It's easy to look at this life and say we're learning from it when we're part of the white American middle-class. What about children who starve to death? What did they learn? The only thing we can say about such a scenario is that it is grossly unjust! Our hearts cry out for justice!

In a scenario where God never brings justice, the responsible parties will never be accountable. What possible reason is there for this version of hell on earth?

People hold to the view that God will never bring justice because they can't stand the thought of a judging God. A judging God is incompatible with their views of love. "God is supposed to be loving, so how could he ever judge anyone?" they wonder. But in fact this view creates an unloving, unfair God—a God who puts people through a life of suffering for no reason! These are very serious problems. Once again, people haven't thought through all the implications. They latch on to ideas because they sound good without thinking them through to the end.

Good and evil are relative.

Others deal with the issue of justice by saying moral categories are things we just make up. In reality, there is no such thing as good or evil. It is all just part of the picture of life. Obviously this would eliminate the problem of judgment altogether since there is neither right or wrong.

Views like this trace their origin to eastern religions like Hinduism and Buddhism. Generally speaking, in the Eastern religious teaching a person will never stand before God and give an account for their life. The Eastern view of God is not of a personal God you can meet face to face. They see God as a life-force that pervades the universe. It isn't appropriate to call God "he" in the eastern philosophy; "it" is a more accurate term. All the actions and things of life are part of God. God is in everything and animates everything.

People in the West have adopted these ideas. Much of what we call "New Age" religion is just Americanized Hinduism or Buddhism. We hear this perspective when people say, "What's wrong? And what's right? Who can tell? Aren't right and wrong just two complementary sides of life?" This is what people are expressing when they say that the things they do will "come back" on them either by reincarnation or in this life. Justice is an impersonal force like gravity rather than the moral decisions of a personal God.

I was talking with a woman who emphasized that she doesn't

believe in things like "sins." "That's a primitive concept to make us feel guilty," she explained. Her morality was based on what "comes naturally." "If we follow our nature and don't hurt the world around us, then we are doing the right thing." This is "Americanized Hinduism." We just try to go with the flow of our deepest nature and the environment we live in.

Different "kinds" of God

This discussion ultimately rests on what kind of God exists. If no God exists, then it is useless to talk about moral categories like right and wrong. If God is more like a life-force than a personal being, perhaps categories like right and wrong are irrelevant. Calling something "wrong" is a reaction from within us as persons. Saying something like love is right is nothing more than a personal comment on a very personal interaction. It takes a personal God to decree that some things are right and some things are wrong. It takes a personal God—someone you have to meet face to face— to exercise judgment.

To think of it another way, you would never be "wrong" for defying a force like gravity. You would never be "right" for submitting to a force. In the Eastern religions, if you act in violation of God (violate the laws of Karma, for example), then equal and opposite forces simply react. If you jump up, you will fall back down. This method of dealing with God's justice is to deny that God is personal. Therefore there is no right or wrong.There will be no ultimate judgment.

The discussion of whether God is personal and therefore able to judge is a topic we will cover under the study of God. However, we could point out a couple things about the existence of a personal God here.

If we assume God exists, where should we look for information on what he is like? How can we tell what characteristics he or it might have? The best place to look is in the world around us. There we see plenty of signs of personality. We see creativity. We see design and intention because things fit together so well and have a purpose. In human beings we see the ultimate manifestations of personality. We have personality. We love, plan, aspire to virtuous things, have aesthetic values, communicate, and have "personality." Where did these things come from? What is their source? The Bible's answer is they are also found in God himself. One thing's for sure—it would be very strange to talk about an impersonal force loving, planning, calling things beautiful, or communicating.

On the level of experience, it is difficult to deny the existence of good and evil. When someone hurts or offends us, we say the act was "wrong." When we see gross violations like murder or rape, imagine saying, "That's just part of the give and take of life." It's the same when disaster strikes. In this view, a disease like AIDS is just as much a part of God as a beautiful day!

If we go back to the source of this form of thought, we learn it is not without some form of ultimate justice. It is not a personal justice where we meet a final judge face to face. It is an impersonal law of retribution called the "karmic laws" in Hindu thought. The idea is that the things we do will come back on us. For every action there is a reaction. If we jump up, we'll come back down.

The teaching of reincarnation ties into this system of justice. If a person is born into a very harsh environment and has a hard life, it is because of things he or she has done in previous lives. This is very hard for me to accept. It's hard for me to say that if someone is starving, that must be their role in life. If someone is raped, it's just karmic law exacting its form of justice. My problem is not with the notion of justice itself. My problem is that such justice leaves little incentive to do anything in this world. Life becomes the arena for judgment—once again a version of hell on earth. It leaves me with an unsettling sense of fatalism.

In the end, these questions depend on what kind of God actually exists. If God is impersonal, justice is simply a matter of impersonal and inflexible laws that govern the universe. If God is personal, justice will be settled at the discretion of a person. He will pass judgment on the things that have happened in this life. These questions will be more thoroughly addressed when we study God's nature.

The Bible's answer: Impartial justice

Now that we've looked at some other possible solutions to the problem of sin and justice, it's time to consider the Bible's answer.

The standard is perfection.

The Bible's answer to where God draws the line on sins is quite different from the religious approach. The Bible says God's standard is perfection. Even one sin is too many. I appreciate the way James says it in James 2:10:

> For whoever keeps the whole law and yet stumbles at just one point is guilty of breaking all of it.

The "law" is the written standard we find in the Old Testament.

The most famous part of the law is the Ten Commandments—things like "Do not steal" and "Do not lie." James says the whole thing is like a chain and if you break one link, it's broken. That's it.

It is ridiculous to think of anyone breaking just one of God's standards. The tenth commandment, for example, says we should not covet things that aren't ours (Ex. 20:17). James explains that coveting other people's things is wrong (e.g. their money, their spouse) because it leads to strife, hatred, and even murder. But who doesn't long for things that don't rightfully belong to them? Who doesn't plot how to get them? If I could honestly track my own thought life, a huge chunk of it would be consumed with greedy and envious thoughts.

Maybe some of us feel like we don't covet very much. But what about the way Jesus explained the law when an inquiring man asked:

> "Teacher, which is the great commandment in the Law?" And he [Jesus] said to him, "'You shall love the Lord your God with all your heart, and with all your soul, and with all your mind.' This is the great and foremost commandment. The second is like it, 'You shall love your neighbor as yourself.' On these two commandments depend the whole Law and the Prophets" (Matt. 22:36-40).

Here are two of God's commands that are active. In other words, it's not, 'avoid this and stay away from that.' Here is the challenge for people who think they don't covet or don't lie. *Do* you love God with all your heart, soul, and mind? *Do* you love your neighbor as yourself? This isn't just a matter of waving to your neighbor when you see him. We do a lot of things for ourselves. We go out of our way for ourselves. We sacrifice for ourselves. When we make a mistake, we forgive ourselves. Is this how we love other people?

When asked to clarify this point, Jesus told a story about a man who was badly beaten by robbers. As he lay on the road, a priest walked by but didn't help because he was afraid it would make him ritually unclean. Then another very religious man passed by and avoided the stricken man. Finally, a Samaritan came along. Samaritans were hated by the Jews Jesus was talking to because they didn't practice the right kind of religion. But this Samaritan showed mercy and went out of his way for someone who was his enemy (see Luke 10:30–37). That was Jesus' response to people who wanted to water things down by narrowing the term "neighbor"—Jesus taught God's ideal was to love and forgive enemies. He was exposing the religious types who thought they had very little problem with sin.

This is an example of how piercing God's instructions are. They are aimed at our hearts. It is truly ridiculous to think of only sinning a few times in a lifetime. Every human being sins countless times. God is just doing the only thing that makes sense. Instead of drawing some arbitrary line and saying, "10,000 sins and you're OK, 10,001 and you go to hell," he says, "everyone is in the same boat." When we try to tell the difference between people on the moral scale, the distinctions become too fuzzy.

Obviously, when it comes to the effect of sins in this life, some are worse than others. We can say it is worse to kill someone than to hate him. But this is focusing on the effect of the sin. God is in the position of looking at the scope of a person's whole life with thousands and thousands of injustices. He has to say, "Every single person is wrong." In comparison to his own perfect character, we all are completely corrupt.

All have sinned and fall short of the glory of God (Rom. 3:23).

Justice must be served.

Then there is the problem of bringing judgment on people even when you love them. This brings us to the problem of what God should do about sin in the light of his absolute, pure love for us. He completely loves people but the things they do are wrong and cry out for justice. What should he do?

First of all, God is not under obligation to do anything. He could be loving and yet judge every single human being who has ever lived. The biblical teaching of human choice tells us that people have chosen to reject God. People continually choose to reject God. We reject him in the sense that we don't do what he says. We reject him in the sense that we don't seek out his authority in our lives. God could judge the entire human race because of our free will—the choice we have made.

Surely if God is loving and yet judged people he loved, he would be torn apart. His grief would be impossible for us to understand because we always judge people we don't like. Imagine the president's brother committing a serious crime like murder. Then imagine the president exercising his power to grant clemency! He gets his brother off the hook for murder! Not many people would conclude, "Oh, he must really love his brother." What people would say is, "Let's impeach this corrupt president!"

The Bible confirms that God's justice cannot be compromised even if it means judging people he fervently loves. He grieves over the choices we make and the resulting judgment.

Say to them, "As surely as I live, declares the Sovereign Lord, I
take no pleasure in the death of the wicked, but rather that they
turn from their ways and live. Turn! Turn from your evil ways!"
(Ezek. 33:11).

God says that when judgment comes, he will desperately wishes it
hadn't! But he will not pretend. He won't fake it and act as if nothing
is wrong. Jesus wept over people's stubbornness. He wanted them to
receive him and his message but they wouldn't.

O Jerusalem, Jerusalem, you who kill the prophets and stone those
sent to you, how often I have longed to gather your children together,
as a hen gathers her chicks under her wings, but you were not willing.
Look, your house is left to you desolate. For I tell you, you will not
see me again until you say, "Blessed is he who comes in the name of
the Lord." (Matt. 23:37–39).

Jesus was distressed at the unwillingness of the people. By saying,
"Your house is left to you desolate," he is saying that they have chosen
God's rejection.

So justice with God is completely impartial. Everyone is guilty.
Everyone is deserving of judgment because of the choices we have
made. Most importantly, God would still be loving if he uniformly
judged everyone.

This is hard for us because we don't like the thought of being
judged. We don't believe we deserve it. We don't believe some of the
people we love deserve it. For me, this is the hardest part of the
Christian message—I deserve judgment. In my experience, it is the
single greatest barrier that keeps people from listening to the gospel.
If I were an impartial observer and saw the way I have hurt people,
rebelled against my Creator, and lived a life of selfishness, I would
have no problem saying that I deserve judgment. The problem is, it
just doesn't *feel* like it.

We have the problem of "sloganeering." We have little slogans we
throw around in our minds but they may have nothing to do with reality.
"I'm basically a good person," is one of them. "I've tried to be good to
others" or "I try to follow the Golden Rule" are other examples. Slogans
like these are numbing. They help us pretend nothing is wrong.

This is why Jesus Christ and other biblical figures worked to expose
the truth of our sinfulness. When we see the truth about ourselves,
there is hope because we are ready for God's solution. God has
provided us with a means of escape from judgment.

A surprise substitute!

But God has made it possible for someone else to "serve our sentence." God's justice cannot be ignored. Yet because of His intense love for us, he has provided a substitute. That substitute was none other than Jesus Christ. Jesus was born into this world for the purpose of becoming a sacrifice for us.

Our sins must be punished but the punishment fell on an innocent substitute who voluntarily took our place. It was a complete surprise because there is nothing in God's love or God's justice that necessitates such a move. He could have simply judged us and left it at that. Instead he came up with an answer nobody would have guessed.

Before Christ came, the Bible foretold and illustrated the idea of a substitute in many different ways. One illustration came from the life of Abraham. He was the father of the Jewish people through whom Jesus the Messiah came.

One of the puzzling stories in the Bible is in Genesis 22 involving Abraham and his son Isaac. It is a story that has often confused Bible readers. God came to Abraham and told him to kill his only son and offer him up as a sacrifice. An instruction like this wouldn't seem too shocking if Abraham had come from a culture that regularly practiced human sacrifice. But the God of the Bible had made it clear over and over again that he abhors that kind of thing! In fact, he instructed the Israelites that anyone practicing human sacrifice deserves the death penalty! (Deut. 18:10).

Here was the loving God telling Abraham to kill his son. God knew how powerful the request was because he said to Abraham, "Take your son, *your only son*, Isaac, *whom you love*, and go to the region of Moriah. Sacrifice him there as a burnt offering on one of the mountains I will tell you about" (Gen. 22:2). "Take the one you love," God said.

The striking part of the story is that Abraham obeyed God. He set off on a three-day journey to the region of Moriah. I can't imagine what thoughts went through his mind during that time. Hebrews tells us that Abraham believed God would raise his son from the dead (see Heb. 11:19). Abraham must have believed something like that because he said to his servants, "*We* will return to you" (Gen. 22:5). To say the least, the story downplays Abraham's turmoil.

When Abraham reached Moriah, he demonstrated his willingness to go all the way to obey God. He got out a knife and prepared to plunge it into the heart of his only son. But God stopped him!

Abraham looked up and there in a thicket he saw a ram caught by its horns. He went over and took the ram and sacrificed it as a burnt offering instead of his son. So Abraham called that place The Lord Will Provide. And to this day it is said, "On the mountain of the Lord it will be provided" (Gen. 22:13–14).

God illustrated two powerful lessons that day. For one, he illustrated that there will come a day when he will provide a substitute for us. He will make it so we don't have to die. This is the great surprise! It is an interesting *coincidence* in history that the mountain Abraham ascended to sacrifice Isaac is the same mountain upon which Jerusalem was later built. Of course Jesus, God's provision, was sacrificed in Jerusalem. The saying in verse 14 turned out to be a remarkable prophecy.

Secondly, God illustrated just how powerful the sacrifice of Jesus will be. The love between the members of the Trinity is perfect— stronger than between a father and his only son. But when Jesus went to the cross for us, nobody yelled, "Stop!" God endured the pain of seeing his Son die for our sins.

The Substitute was a surprise. Now we need to look at how such a substitution works.

Jesus died for God's justice

No event has changed history as much as the death of Jesus Christ. Why was it so powerful? The Bible looks to it as the focal point of all history.

This most powerful event has been interpreted many different ways. Some have emphasized the fact that the cross meant great suffering. Jesus truly suffered for us, so we should be inspired to respond to God. The Bible certainly teaches this. Peter tells us we were bought by the shed blood of Christ:

> For you know that it was not with perishable things such as silver or gold that you were redeemed from the empty way of life handed down to you from your forefathers, but with the precious blood of Christ, a lamb without blemish or defect. (1 Peter 1:18–19)

Peter emphasizes the great cost Jesus paid to be our substitute. His point is that God's love should move us to respond to him.

Others have seen the victory in the death of Christ. Jesus was put to death by those who rejected him, as well as the spiritual beings who were at war with him. But he rose again! The powers of death couldn't hold him down. He conquered death, Satan, and sin. The cross of Christ was a victorious turning point in history.

But first and foremost, the death of Christ was to satisfy God's justice. We have a hard time believing that we deserve judgment. As far as we're concerned, God could just forgive us and that would be fine. Yet it wouldn't be fine from God's point of view. He cannot ignore his justice. This is why Christ died. Other perspectives on the cross are mere side-effects.

Substitution at the cross

Jesus was a substitute for us. He died in our place. That is as simply as it can be stated.

Some have argued against the notion of substitution. It is puzzling to them how one person could die for another. Others take offense at the fact that God's justice demands the death of anyone. It seems barbaric—a throwback to pagan ritual.

We will consider these objections, but first we need to see that it is impossible to get away from the notion of substitution in the Bible. From the time of Moses, God taught his people that they needed a substitute. As an object lesson, he set up an animal sacrifice system that revolved around worship in the tabernacle.

In Leviticus 16 God prescribed a ceremony that foreshadowed what Christ would do. He told the priest to select two goats, one to be killed and the other to be sent out into the wilderness. The goat that was killed was called a "sin offering" meaning it was killed for the sins of the people. The priest then took some of the blood from the goat and brought it into a small room in the temple called the "Holy of Holies." There was a box in the center of the room called the "Ark of the Covenant." It had two statues of angels looking down at it. The Ark contained the tablets of the Ten Commandments and several other items that represented the sins of the people. A priest sprinkled the blood over this box, symbolizing that the sins of the people were covered by the death of the substitute.

To make things even more clear, the other goat, called the "scapegoat," was brought to the priest. The priest laid his hands on the goat and confessed the sins of the people. The goat was then driven out into the wilderness. The imagery taught that a substitute could take the sins of the people away, far away. Some Jewish traditions tell us the goat was even pushed over a cliff to make sure it never came back.

These rituals were only pictures of the real thing. The genuine article came later in the substitutionary sacrifice of Jesus. As it says in Hebrews:

The law is only a shadow of the good things that are coming—not the realities themselves. For this reason it can never, by the same sacrifices repeated endlessly year after year, make perfect those who draw near to worship (Heb. 10:1).

Obviously an animal couldn't be a substitute for a person. But Jesus, who was fully human and fully God, was the perfect sacrifice. As it says later in the same chapter:

By one sacrifice he has made perfect forever those who are being made holy (Heb. 10:14).

"Those who are being made holy" is a biblical term for anyone who puts their faith in God (see Eph. 1:4; Col. 3:12). It's a term that is often translated as "saints." This verse says that Jesus' one sacrifice was adequate to substitute for all the sins of those who believe in him.

Other passages make it clear that the guilt of our sins was placed on Christ. And they are not just New Testament passages either. The Old Testament taught that the rituals performed in the temple predicted the coming Savior. One of the clearest Old Testament predictions of Christ's work puts it this way:

Surely our griefs he himself bore. And our sorrows he carried. Yet we ourselves esteemed him stricken, smitten of God, and afflicted.

But he was pierced through for our transgressions. He was crushed for our iniquities. The chastening for our well-being fell upon him. And by his scourging we are healed.

All of us like sheep have gone astray. Each of us has turned to his own way. But the Lord has caused the iniquity of us all to fall on him (Isa. 53:4–6 NASB).

Isaiah is portraying the idea of substitution in many different ways. The coming Messiah would pay the price for our sins. Some other verses on the substitutionary nature of Christ's death are 2 Corinthians 5:21, Matthew 20:28, Mark 10:45, and Galatians 3:13.

Clearly the Bible teaches substitution. But what about these objections I mentioned earlier? How can one person die for another? Isn't this a barbaric notion of appeasing the wrath of the gods by human sacrifice?

It is difficult to accept that one person can take the punishment of another. People have stumbled over this point for centuries. However, we should realize the ultimate Judge in the universe is God. He is the one who has the ability to say what is fair and unfair. If, in his economy, it is allowable for one person to pay the price for another, that is his prerogative.

We have already been introduced to this feature of God's justice. Adam and Eve were representatives of the entire human race. Their decision had an effect on all of us. In the cross, Jesus was the representative for the entire human race. His obedience has an effect on whoever decides to accept it (see Rom. 5:18).

Secondly, Jesus' sacrifice was voluntary. He freely chose to lay down his life for us. He wasn't a random whipping-boy selected to receive our punishment. He intensely loved us and stepped forward to volunteer. In Jesus' own words:

> No one takes [my life] from me, but I lay it down of my own accord. I have authority to lay it down and authority to take it up again (John 10:18).

Many other passages emphasize this free choice of Jesus to lay down his life for people he loves (See Phil. 2:5–8; John 15:13). I think this sheds a different light on the subject. It might be something akin to a parent paying a ticket for a child. But obviously, all such comparisons fall way short of the actual picture.

On the issue that the sacrifice of Jesus seems barbaric, the answer will become clear as we look at the words used to describe the death of Christ.

Different terms for the death of Christ
Propitiation / Atonement
One descriptive word for Christ's work on the Cross is *propitiation* (also translated as atonement). The key places this word is found are Romans 3:25, Hebrews 2:17, 1 John 2:2, and 4:10. The term came from pagan religious rites. It means "to satisfy" or "appease." In non-Christian rituals, pagans might offer a god an animal or the fruit of one's labors or even a human being to appease his anger.

There is an important difference between the biblical use of this term and the way other religions use it. In the other religions, the propitiation of a sacrifice was intended to turn the gods' anger into favor. In other words, a god would be angry and about to judge the people but a sacrifice would avert the anger temporarily. The Bible on the other hand teaches us that God has *always* loved us. The propitiation of Jesus Christ was *because* God loved us. He loved us just as much as before Christ died as after. As 1 John 4:10 says:

> This is love: not that we loved God, but that he loved us and sent his Son as an *atoning sacrifice* (propitiation) for our sins.

What changed was not the turning of God's anger into love like the other non-Christian rituals of the day taught. It was that God's justice was satisfied. The sacrifice of Christ satisfied (propitiated) God's impartial justice.

Reconciliation

Reconciliation has to do with bringing together estranged parties. Usually reconciliation implies hostility. Several passages teach the work of the Cross as reconciliation.

> And although you were formerly alienated and hostile in mind, engaged in evil deeds, yet He has now reconciled you in His fleshly body through death, in order to present you before Him holy and blameless and beyond reproach (Col. 1:21–22 NASB).

It is interesting to note that the Bible never talks about God being reconciled to us as if we were the ones holding a grudge (see also 2 Cor. 5:18–20; Eph. 2:13–14; Rom. 5:1–10). It is always humans being reconciled back to God. This imagery teaches us that the barrier was on God's side of the conflict! Paul describes Christ's work on the Cross as "canceling out a certificate of debt filled with judgments that were hostile towards us" (Col. 2:14). God in his perfect justice was angry at the sin in our lives.

As far as we are concerned, it would be fine if God simply forgave us—if he just let bygones be bygones. Sure, we have hostility or frustration with God in our hearts. We still don't think that should come between us. We're willing to let things slide when it comes to judgment. But that's not possible from his perspective. He can't ignore his justice. God had to overcome the barrier of our sin before we could be reconciled. Again we see the Cross had its effect on the justice of God.

Redemption

The death of Christ is referred to as "redemption" or a "ransom" in passages such as Matthew 20:28:

The Son of Man did not come to be served, but to serve and give his life a ransom for many (see also Mark 10:45, Gal. 3:13, Heb. 9:15, Eph. 1:7, and 1 Peter 1:18–19).

These terms speak of deliverance by a payment. The Bible portrays people in bondage and Christ paid to set us free. An interesting question to consider is to whom was the price paid? There was a strong tradition in the early church that taught that God actually paid off Satan who owned the whole world. This is difficult to see, however, because Satan is a usurper and a thief. He is no rightful owner of anything.

As we examine this question we should not push the metaphor too far. The notion of redemption communicates that Jesus paid a high price for us (1 Peter 1:18–19). It also communicates the idea of substitution again as Jesus substituted himself to redeem us.

Conclusion

With these pictures of the death of Christ we have an idea of what happened at the Cross. Now we need to look at how the work of the cross applies to us.

Study summary

Key Points

- There must be justice because of sin. God's sense of justice is not like ours; he is absolutely fair. We might draw the line arbitrarily, excusing our own sins and wanting punishment for those worse than us. But God's impartial justice sees all sin as worthy of punishment.
- There are several classic ways religious people deal with the problem of sin and justice. Some believe that God will draw distinctions between people, punishing some and not others based on their moral differences. Others believe God will forgive everyone and there will be no punishment for sin. A third group downplay the distinction between good and evil. All of these alternatives present serious problems.
- God's answer to the problem of sin and justice is to be absolutely fair. He sees even one sin as too many (see James 2:10).
- On the other hand, God loves humans even though we are all worthy of His judgment. The answer he provided was completely surprising. Jesus Christ gave his life as a substitute for us so that we could be forgiven.
- There are numerous words and metaphors which describe Jesus'

death on the cross which point to the substitutionary nature of
his sacrifice.

Key Scriptures
- James 2:10
- Romans 3:23
- 1 Peter 1:18–19
- Hebrews 10:14
- Isaiah 53
- 2 Corinthians 5:21
- 1 John 4:10
- Colossians 1:21–22
- Matthew 20:28

Important Terms
- Substitution
  Christ received God's judgment in our place. Christ gave his
  life as a substitute for us. We deserved judgment but he took it
  in our place.

- Propitiation
  The satisfaction or appeasement of God's justice. The sacrifice
  of Christ was enough to satisfy the just punishment for the sins
  of the entire world.

- Atonement
  The peace with God we have because Christ died for us. Since
  God's justice is satisfied by the death of Christ, the rift between
  God and sinful humans is bridged.

- Reconciliation
  The broken relationship between God and us is healed. The rift
  between God and humans could not be bridged as long as the
  problem of sin remained.

- Redemption
  Paying the price for sin. Jesus paid an enormous price by dying
  for us his work on the Cross is sometimes described as "buying
  us" or "redemption."

For Further Reading
- *The Atonement* by Leon Morris, InterVarsity, 1983
- *Redemption: Accomplished and Applied* by John Murray, Wm. B. Eerdmans, 1955

CHAPTER FIVE

TURNING TO GOD

How to receive God's forgiveness

We have looked at how Jesus' death satisfies the justice of God so he can offer us his forgiveness. The question we will look at now is why that forgiveness applies to some people but not others.

The answer to this question given in the Bible is a heart attitude of faith. A person can receive God's forgiveness by believing that he wants to give it to them. On the other hand, if a person refuses to believe in God's provision, their guilt remains. That always sounds a bit theoretical but it helps to look at the different terms and metaphors the Bible uses to describe saving faith.

Faith / Belief

One of the main terms the Bible uses to describe the attitude God is looking for in us is "faith." The same Greek and Hebrew words are translated as both "faith" and "belief" in English.

John uses this term in his Gospel of Jesus' life 100 times. He records Jesus talking about the need for faith in order to receive forgiveness. Some of these sayings are the most powerful in the whole Bible on the topic of salvation. They're great for memorizing and sharing with people who wonder about the Bible's message.

John 3:16

For God so loved the world that he gave his one and only Son, that whoever believes in him shall not perish but have eternal life.

This is one of the clearest expressions of what it means to believe in Jesus Christ. That's why it is has been a favorite memory verse for so long. When John says "God gave his Son," he is understating the fact that Jesus came to die. If we believe Jesus' death was for us then God grants us "eternal life."

The power of John's description lies in its simplicity. God has made his salvation so simple and accessible—anyone can understand it.

John 5:24
> I tell you the truth, whoever hears my word and believes him who sent me has eternal life and will not be condemned; he has crossed over from death to life.

Here is another simple yet powerful statement about faith. Jesus says that the object of faith must be God the Father. What does it mean to believe in God? Does it mean simply to believe God exists? Actually, it's much more than that. James points out that even God's spiritual enemies, demons, believe he exists.

> You believe that there is one God. Good! Even the demons believe that—and shudder (James 2:19).

So "believing in God" must mean more than just believing he exists. Hebrews tells us that it means believing he loves us and wants to save us.

> And without faith it is impossible to please God, because anyone who comes to him must believe that he exists and that he rewards those who earnestly seek him (Heb. 11:6).

He is telling us we must also believe in God's love and saving goodness. If we seek him out, which is a good way to define faith, God will reward us with his salvation. To believe in God is to believe he is there and he loves us. It is to believe he wants to save us with his forgiveness.

There are also passages in John that describe the consequences of unbelief.

John 3:18
> Whoever believes in him is not judged, but whoever does not believe stands condemned already because he has not believed in the name of God's one and only Son.

Believing in Jesus means forgiveness and an escape from God's judgment. However, the guilt remains with a person who won't believe. The difference between the two people is not how guilty they are but whether they have dealt with their guilt by faith.

Receive

Another term the Bible uses to describe our response to God is "receiving." John 1:12–13 explains:

> Yet to all who received him, to those who believed in his name, he gave the right to become children of God—children born not of natural descent, nor of human decision or a husband's will, but born of God.

We see that the notion of "receiving" is parallel to "believing." This is also where we get the popular term "accepting Christ." The idea is that we accept what he has done as applying to us but we also accept him as a person to come and live within us and change us.

Ask / Seek

Ultimately, if we believe in God's gift of forgiveness, we will seek it out somehow. We have already seen this in Hebrews 11:6, where faith was defined both as believing God exists and his being a rewarder of those who seek him. Biblical faith means that we believe God has good gifts for us if we take them.

Jesus explains this in Luke 11:9–10:

> So I say to you: Ask and it will be given to you; seek and you will find; knock and the door will be opened to you. For everyone who asks receives; he who seeks finds; and to him who knocks, the door will be opened.

Here are the practicals of faith. We have to talk to God. We have to pray. It comes down to our communicating with God to express our faith. Jesus concludes his promise by saying:

> Which of you fathers, if your son asks for a fish, will give him a snake instead? Or if he asks for an egg, will give him a scorpion? If you then, though you are evil, know how to give good gifts to your children, how much more will your Father in heaven give the Holy Spirit to those who ask him! (Luke 11:11–13).

The giving of the Holy Spirit is a sign of our forgiveness as we will discuss in the next chapter. Jesus assures us that if we seek him we will receive his salvation.

Turn

A term that has become popular with preachers of the gospel is "repent." It has come to have some negative connotations because some preachers use it to badger people about their sins. Most people think that repent means they have to be extremely sorry about the sins they have done.

But the term itself means simply "turn" or "change of mind." In the Old Testament repent meant to "turn to God" for help or salvation. In Ezekiel 18:32, God says:

> For I take no pleasure in the death of anyone, declares the Sovereign Lord. Repent and live!

God is calling for people to turn to him for salvation. "Turning" also implies rejecting whatever we were putting our faith in, in place of God. If we had been looking to other gods for salvation, then we must turn from them. If we had been trusting in ourselves for the things God should provide, then we must now admit we were wrong.

There are people who take the concept of "repentance" and construe it to mean that in order to be forgiven, we must completely desert our past life. They see repentance as more than changing the object of our faith. They see it as a complete life change. It is unwise to take the picture of "turning" too far. For example, I might realize that my lifestyle is wrong. I have lived in rebellion against God and I need forgiveness. That would be repentance. I would be "changing my mind" about my life. Before I thought it was OK, maybe even the best way to live. Now I realize it was so wrong—it was worthy of God's judgment.

Does that mean I will never again do the things I have done before? The reality is, in action I may continue to stumble in many ways. But now I have a different perspective on my sin than before.

I don't want to minimize the change of perspective that does take place with repentance. It is a complete turnaround to go from enjoying sin and seeing it as a way of life to the point where we say, "I was so far in the wrong that I deserved God's judgment!" Repentance does create a hunger for change because it involves a shift in our view of sin. Sin is now something harmful, something we need forgiveness for.

There is no doubt, people who turn to God change. The danger I am addressing is *extremism*, which teaches that a person has to completely desert their former lifestyle or they aren't truly saved. Their mistake is taking the metaphor of "turning" to an extreme—applying it to every action they ever do.

"Turning" is just another picture for the concept of faith. It means to turn from self-reliance to dependence on God. Peter used the term in one of his speeches:

> Repent, then, and turn to God, so that your sins may be wiped out, that times of refreshing may come from the Lord (Acts 3:19).

This passage is an excellent description of faith. Peter is emphatically calling on people to put their trust in God for forgiveness. "Turning to him" conjures up images of depending on him, calling out to him, running to him.

Confess

A passage in Romans uses the term "confess" to describe what we must do to obtain salvation.

> If you confess with your mouth, "Jesus is Lord," and believe in your heart that God raised him from the dead, you will be saved (Rom. 10:9).

Believing in Jesus' resurrection is the same as believing that he paid the price for our sins. Paul says earlier in Romans:

> He was delivered over to death for our sins and was raised to life for our forgiveness (Rom. 4:25).

Paul is saying that the evidence of our forgiveness is that Jesus came back from the grave. He has completely paid for all our sins. So it makes perfect sense to say we that must believe Jesus has been raised from the dead. Otherwise, how would we know our sins are forgiven?

It's interesting that he says we must "confess with our mouth, Jesus is Lord." Is this some kind of formula? Is it something that should be said aloud at church? Is it a ritual?

The answer is in the next verse:

> For it is with your heart that you believe and are forgiven, and it is with your mouth that you confess and are saved (Rom. 10:10).

The point is no different from the one we made earlier: If you believe in your heart that God wants to forgive you, you will go to him in prayer to seek it. The term "confess" means to "agree" with God. The idea is that I go to God in prayer and acknowledge he is my Lord, he is my God, and I need his forgiveness. Prior to salvation, we all take a stand that we don't need God. We live our lives independently of him. That is the nature of sin. To confess that he is our Lord is to admit that we need him, we are wrong to be without his authority, and we want to set things right.

Here again, some go to extremes on what it means to confess Jesus is Lord. They insist this is an attitude that should translate into our every action. "If you believe he is Lord, then you'll act like it," they say. But we don't have to live very long to know that people don't act consistently with what they know to be true. The very act of seeking God's forgiveness implies that he has authority over our lives. That doesn't mean from now on I will always live in total submission to him. I may acknowledge he has the right to rule but still try to run things myself. The truth is, this is precisely what we all do. When we talk about spiritual growth later, we'll discuss how we can become more and more consistent in our faithfulness to God.

Confessing is agreeing with God that he is God and I'm not. It's to agree that because of his authority, I have sinned against him and need his forgiveness. It is something that should happen in prayer between God and myself. As Paul says later in the same chapter, "Everyone who calls on the name of the Lord will be saved" (v. 13). Again, there is no doubt that this is an incredible change of heart: to go from one who rules to one who bows the knee and says, "I need your forgiveness! I have sinned against you!" Every time I see someone make that transition I'm stunned.

Why is it so hard to have faith?

We have looked at faith and repentance. Faith is believing in God's goodness and God's love. The natural result of believing in God's goodness is to seek him out. That's why the Bible teaches that faith involves seeking God. Repentance describes the change from placing faith in yourself or something else to placing your faith in God.

Everyone has faith in something. Everyone believes in something for meaning, direction, and morality. So what makes it so hard to place our faith in God? We don't have to do anything, like change the way we dress or talk. We don't have to go through any embarrassing ritual; it's just a prayer of faith between ourselves and God. What is it that makes faith in God so difficult?

The answer in a nutshell is that faith may be simple but it's not easy. There are a some good reasons why faith is difficult.

It's hard to believe.

For one thing, it's just plain hard to believe anything so great as God's complete forgiveness is free. People say, "You mean I can just ask for God's forgiveness and that's all? No way. There has to be a catch. Where's the fine print?"

This skepticism is related to our own character. The saying, "If it seems too good to be true, it is," is generally true. But it's different when we're dealing with God! The Bible describes the free gift of God as God's "graciousness" or God's "grace."

God's grace is a concept that comes up about 150 times in the New Testament alone. The term "grace" can refer to several different ideas but when it is used in connection with salvation it means "favor" or "gift." It is synonymous with God's love. Let's look at the term in a few passages.

Ephesians 2:8–9

> For it is by grace you have been saved, through faith—and this not from yourselves, it is the gift of God—not by works, so that no one can boast.

Paul is saying that salvation is a complete gift we obtained by just believing. When he says we were saved by God's grace, it means we were saved because of God's love. To make it obvious, Paul says the gift of salvation was not given because of "works." Works are simply good deeds people do in order to be noticed or accepted by God. We'll talk about this contrast more in the next section.

Romans 3:24

> And [we] are justified freely by his grace through the redemption that came by Christ Jesus.

Here again Paul is emphasizing that forgiveness is free because of God's grace. Grace is synonymous with God's love. It is also emphasizing a certain aspect of God's love—that it is free and unconditional.

"Grace" is contrasted with "law."

To draw out the notion of God's grace further, we can look at how it is contrasted with "law." Paul often puts these two terms in opposition. For example, in Galatians 2:21, Paul says:

I do not set aside the grace of God, for if righteousness could be gained through the law, Christ died for nothing!

God's grace is the free gift of forgiveness purchased by Jesus' death. The law, which was never intended to save or impart eternal life, is misused by some as a source of God's forgiveness. This is an approach most religions take, where people try to be good enough by their religious deeds and obedience. Paul is saying that a person can try to approach God on the basis of law—doing the right things. Or he can approach God on the basis of God's free gift—apart from any deeds, good or bad. It is one or the other, not both. If we could be acceptable to God based on our deeds, then it was useless for Christ to die. God could simply say, "Here, live up to these standards and you'll make it."

The biblical teaching of grace is hard for us. It's hard to imagine that there is *nothing* I can do to earn God's favor. It's also hard to think anything is *completely* free.

This leads us to our second reason faith is difficult.

Salvation requires humility.

The entire notion of God's grace implies I am unworthy. It means there is nothing about me that says I deserve God's forgiveness. It's a tough pill to swallow. It's also offensive.

Most people would like to think they are good, at least better than others. Perhaps they are more worthy of God's love than others. But the teaching of forgiveness—God's grace—means every human is in the same boat. It says all our good deeds don't even matter!

We should look at a some Scriptures that make this point as clearly as possible.

Ephesians 2:8–9

For it is by grace you have been saved, through faith—and this not from yourselves, it is the gift of God—not by works, so that no one can boast.

We discussed this passage in the last section. Here I want to focus on the last line which gets right to the heart of the matter, "Not by works, so that no one can boast." There is no room for spiritual back-patting with God's grace. And yet this is what some people have lived their whole lives for! They've attended charities, gone to church, given money, all to feel better about themselves! Ephesians 2:9 says it's all worthless when it comes to God's forgiveness.

It's not like everyone consciously wants to boast about their goodness. For most, they just want to avoid saying, "I'm as undeserving as anyone else. I should be judged too." Who wants to view themselves like that?

Galatians 2:16

We . . . know that a man is not justified (forgiven) by observing the law, but by faith in Jesus Christ. So we, too, have put our faith in Christ Jesus that we may be justified by faith in Christ and not by observing the law, because by observing the law no one will be justified.

Paul is saying that no matter how good someone is, he will never be good enough. There is no such thing as a person who will be forgiven by God on the basis of how good he or she has been. It just won't happen. Imagine how distasteful this is to a person who has tried their whole life to do the right thing?

Luke 7:36-50

There is a great story in Luke about Jesus when he was eating at a religious person's house. This incident illustrates the offense that God's forgiveness causes.

Now one of the Pharisees invited Jesus to have dinner with him, so he went to the Pharisee's house and reclined at the table. When a woman who had lived a sinful life in that town learned that Jesus was eating at the Pharisee's house, she brought an alabaster jar of perfume, and as she stood behind him at his feet weeping, she began to wet his feet with her tears. Then she wiped them with her hair, kissed them and poured perfume on them.

When the Pharisee who had invited him saw this, he said to himself, "If this man were a prophet, he would know who is touching him and what kind of woman she is—that she is a sinner."

Jesus answered him, "Simon, I have something to tell you."

"Tell me, teacher," he said.

"Two men owed money to a certain moneylender. One owed him five hundred denarii, and the other fifty. Neither of them had the money to pay him back, so he canceled the debts of both. Now which of them will love him more?"

Simon replied, "I suppose the one who had the bigger debt canceled."

"You have judged correctly," Jesus said.

Then he turned toward the woman and said to Simon, "Do you see this woman? I came into your house. You did not give me any water for my feet, but she wet my feet with her tears and wiped them with her hair. You did not give me a kiss, but this woman, from the time I entered, has not stopped kissing my feet. You did not put oil on my head, but she has poured perfume on my feet. Therefore, I tell you, her many sins have been forgiven—for she loved much. But he who has been forgiven little loves little."

Then Jesus said to her, "Your sins are forgiven."

The other guests began to say among themselves, "Who is this who even forgives sins?"

Jesus said to the woman, "Your faith has saved you; go in peace."

What a perfect picture of religious pride versus humility! The absolute forgiveness of God requires our humility, so it offends people who feel like they don't need it. On the one hand, the man who had worked diligently to be upright was judging this lady, whom he referred to as a "sinner." He was not grateful for Christ's message of forgiveness, because he thought he deserved it! She, on the other hand, knew she deserved nothing but judgment. Her joy at hearing that Jesus would accept her and love her drove her to this emotional eruption. It's hard to appreciate this woman's feelings unless you have experienced the deepest sense of unworthiness. Usually when we have such feelings, we work hard to forget them. The lesson of this passage is that when we lose touch with our unworthiness and failure, then we become snooty and self-righteous.

Jesus notes in verse 50 that hers was an attitude of faith. Faith, humility, and gratitude go hand in hand.

1 Peter 5:5

All of you, clothe yourselves with humility toward one another, because, "God opposes the proud but gives grace to the humble."

Peter quotes an Old Testament passage but the principle is timeless: God's grace is for those who know they don't deserve it. This is at the heart of why I say faith is hard. Biblical faith means humility. It means saying, "I need God completely. There is nothing I can do to earn his love."

When you tell people about the good news of forgiveness, you will see them get right up to the point of receiving forgiveness but stumble on this issue. Because of pride, they only want it if they can pay for it.

What happens when we are forgiven?

The next thing to look at is what happens when we receive God's forgiveness. Here again are some powerful biblical stories, words, and metaphors that communicate this transition.

Justification

One of the main terms used to describe what we have as Christians is "justification." Justification is a term used in courtrooms. It means "acquitted, found innocent." It is a powerful term because of how complete it is. It's not that we are "good enough." We are innocent! It's not that the charges were dropped. We were acquitted of all charges!

Let's consider some passages that talk about our justification.

Romans 5:1

> Therefore, since we have been justified through faith, we have peace with God through our Lord Jesus Christ.

Since we are innocent, nothing stands between ourselves and God. There is no issue of contention between us. It is one morally innocent person relating to another. I don't think we should just consider this notion of peace as some theological concept either. Peace with God is an experience. People know it and feel it. Time after time, when people turn to God for his forgiveness, they tell me that for the first time in their lives they feel right with God. The same was true for me. Before I turned to God there was a constant sense of irritation, or maybe it was guilt. Before I would go to sleep or early in the morning when I woke up, my mind kept wandering back to the awareness of tension between God and me. But after I experienced peace with God, I had a completely different sense about my life. I felt relieved. I felt thankful. This experience can be interrupted by guilt or other factors. But it is true that new Christians experience a new sense of reconciliation with their Creator.

1 Corinthians 6:9–11

> Do you not know that the wicked will not inherit the kingdom of God? Do not be deceived: Neither the sexually immoral nor idolaters nor adulterers nor male prostitutes nor homosexual offenders nor thieves nor the greedy nor drunkards nor slanderers nor swindlers will inherit the kingdom of God. And that is what some of you were. But you were washed . . . you were justified in the name of the Lord Jesus Christ and by the Spirit of our God.

Here is one of my favorite passages on justification. Paul refers to a whole slew of sinful behaviors. He catches everyone in the net because he doesn't just refer to unusual lifestyles like "male prostitutes." He also refers to greed and slandering (bad-mouthing people), things everyone does.

What makes this passage even more powerful is many of the Corinthians were currently involved in some of these lifestyles. For example, in 1 Corinthians 11 Paul rebukes them for getting drunk during communion! Some of them are also involved in sexual immorality of all kinds. Even so, Paul says, "Such *were* some of you!" They were washed; they were justified. So God doesn't look at them that way anymore. To apply this passage to yourself, just think of some of the things you currently do, like lying or hating or lusting, and realize, "That's how I was! God doesn't even look at me that way anymore!"

Justification has nothing to do with what a person *does*. It has to do with what Christ *has done* for us.

Given the Holy Spirit

A second result of our forgiveness is we receive the Holy Spirit. This is God's Spirit—not a force, but a real person who comes and lives inside us.

Luke 11:13

We looked at this passage under the topic of faith. Jesus promised, "If you then, though you are evil, know how to give good gifts to your children, how much more will your Father in heaven give the Holy Spirit to those who ask him!"

One of the great messages Jesus came to bring was that we could be indwelt by God's Spirit. Previous to the death of Christ, God's Spirit had not actually lived within people. After Christ's death and resurrection, the Spirit came to be with us as a sign of our salvation.

John 7:38–39

"Whoever believes in me, as the Scripture has said, streams of living water will flow from within him." By this he meant the Spirit, whom those who believed in him were later to receive. Up to that time the Spirit had not been given, since Jesus had not yet been glorified.

Jesus brought the promise of restoring our spiritual dimension—reuniting us with God. The implications of God's Spirit living within us are tremendous, as Jesus communicates with the imagery of "streams of living water" welling up within us. I think this speaks of the supernatural, powerful life God intended for us.

Romans 8:16

The Spirit himself testifies with our spirit that we are God's children.

God's Spirit assures us that God forgives and accepts us. As Romans 5:1 states, "We have peace with God." The Holy Spirit communicates this peace to us as an experience. This is why people often relate very powerful feelings of peace, joy, and excitement when they become Christians.

I want to be clear that for some people the new experience of God's Spirit can be more subtle than for others. I have seen some just burst with excitement—a normally reserved man looking for someone to hug—at the first experience of God's Spirit. I have also seen some whose experience is very subtle—maybe a new sense of peace or rightness as we discussed previously. In these cases, God is simply working differently with different people. We can be sure he has good reasons for doing so.

Eternal life

Yet another consequence of our faith in Christ is eternal life. You may remember some of Jesus' promises, such as John 3:16. Once we have been forgiven, there is no judgment to face at the end of history. We simply pass directly into heaven.

Revelation 20:12

And I saw the dead, great and small, standing before the throne, and books were opened. Another book was opened, which is the book of life. The dead were judged according to what they had done as recorded in the books.

This is a powerful image of all the people of the world standing before God. John says that "the books" were opened. These books represent God's knowledge of all the things we have done in life. This is exactly the kind of judgment most people expect from God. They expect him to evaluate their lives and see whether they're good enough.

John says there was another book opened up, the "Book of Life." In this book are the names of all those who have placed their faith in Jesus Christ. These people aren't even questioned. They simply pass into eternal life. If your name is not in the Book of Life, then you'll be judged based on your deeds. John foretells an ominous truth about those who will stand before God and have "the books" opened:

> If anyone's name was not found written in the book of life, he was thrown into the lake of fire (v. 15).

So the alarming news is that if "the book of deeds" is opened about you, you're in trouble. It's ironic that most people conceive of standing before God and having the books opened. This passage tells us that opening the books is a bad sign. Every single person who stands to give an account of their deeds falls short. Everyone loses. The only way past judgment is to be in the Book of Life. The good news is that those who are in the Book of Life simply pass by and are not judged!

John 5:24

We may recall the words of Christ on this same issue:

> Truly, truly, I say to you, he who hears My word, and believes Him who sent Me, has eternal life, and does not come into judgment, but has passed out of death into life (NASB).

Born Again

There is another picture of what happens to us when we become Christians. We are "born again." This metaphor was first used by Jesus in John 3 with a religious teacher named Nicodemus.

> Now there was a man of the Pharisees named Nicodemus, a member of the Jewish ruling council. He came to Jesus at night and said, "Rabbi, we know you are a teacher who has come from God. For no one could perform the miraculous signs you are doing if God were not with him."
> In reply Jesus declared, "I tell you the truth, no one can see the kingdom of God unless he is born again" (vv. 1–3).

What a mystifying statement! And in fact, that was precisely what Jesus intended. He wanted to throw Nicodemus off by referring to an idea he couldn't possibly understand.

> "How can a man be born when he is old?" Nicodemus asked. "Surely he cannot enter a second time into his mother's womb to be born!"
> Jesus answered, "I tell you the truth, no one can enter the kingdom

of God unless he is born of water and the Spirit. Flesh gives birth to flesh, but the Spirit gives birth to spirit. You should not be surprised at my saying, 'You must be born again.' The wind blows wherever it pleases. You hear its sound, but you cannot tell where it comes from or where it is going. So it is with everyone born of the Spirit."

"How can this be?" Nicodemus asked.

"You are Israel's teacher," said Jesus, "and do you not understand these things?" (vv. 4–10).

Jesus was making Nicodemus realize that salvation is a supernatural gift. It is not something we can do for ourselves. God gives it to us. So Jesus uses a metaphor as perplexing as "born again." The miracle of salvation is no less unbelievable. The approach Jesus took is understandable, considering who Nicodemus was. Here was a religious teacher of Israel who always had the answers. But Jesus was making him realize that he didn't have the answers! He needed what Jesus had.

The notion of being "born again" has become popular as a description of the transition we go through in salvation. Peter describes our salvation experience as being "born again."

Now that you have purified yourselves by obeying the truth so that you have sincere love for your brothers, love one another deeply, from the heart. For you have been born again, not of perishable seed, but of imperishable, through the living and enduring word of God (1 Peter 1:22–23).

Our "obedience to the truth" is the fact that we have received forgiveness. Peter explains that this has an effect on us he calls "purifying," which enables us to sincerely love each other. This transition is so radical, he calls it being "born again."

When God's Spirit comes to live within us, for the first time we have the power to love, the power to follow God, the power to change as we've never had before. This is a decisive change, and the picture of being "born again" is an apt description.

Made Alive / Made New

Along a similar vein, the Bible talks about us being "made new," or "made alive" when we turn to God. One of the best passages on this is 2 Corinthians 5:17:

Therefore, if anyone is in Christ, he is a new creation; the old has gone, the new has come!

This truth is so refreshing for people, it is good to memorize verses like this. God so completely forgives us and accepts us, he sees us as new creatures. This is like the picture painted for us in Psalms 103:12:

> As far as the east is from the west, so far has he removed our transgressions from us.

God also "makes us alive." As Paul simply says:

> When we were dead in our transgressions, He made us alive together with Christ (by grace you have been saved) (Eph. 2:5 NASB).

If you'll recall our study of sin and humans, "death" was separation from God. "Life" is being brought back into fellowship with God. God has restored our spiritual dimension that was lost with Adam and Eve.

Salvation

Finally, we are "saved" when we turn to Christ in faith. Salvation is a term that rubs people the wrong way because it implies we need saving. It implies we were in danger. As we discussed before, the offense of the gospel message is our helplessness. The gospel says that we are in trouble and incapable of saving ourselves.

One of the most clear statements about our need for salvation is Paul's description in Titus 3:3–6:

> For we also once were foolish ourselves, disobedient, deceived, enslaved to various lusts and pleasures, spending our life in malice and envy, hateful, hating one another.
>
> But when the kindness of God our Savior and His love for mankind appeared, He saved us, not on the basis of deeds which we have done in righteousness, but according to His mercy, by the washing of regeneration and renewing by the Holy Spirit, whom He poured out upon us richly through Jesus Christ our Savior (NASB).

God saved us from ourselves! I find a lot in common with Paul's description of life apart from God. It takes brutal honesty to admit you need saving.

Salvation also refers to being spared from God's justice. Jesus explained the choice between facing God's justice and receiving salvation in John 3:17–18:

> For God did not send the Son into the world to judge the world, but
> that the world should be saved through Him.
> He who believes in Him is not judged; he who does not believe has
> been judged already, because he has not believed in the name of the
> only begotten Son of God (NASB).

The choice Jesus describes is between judgment and salvation. If
we believe in God's forgiveness, we have salvation. If we don't, we
face judgment. Again, it's obvious why people don't like the term.
Facing our need for salvation is exactly what is required before we
can have it. I suppose no one will like the term "salvation" until they
are ready to receive it!

Salvation is also a process

Despite the powerful descriptions of those who have faith in God,
many things don't change when we first become Christians. Most of
what God wants to do with us in this life doesn't happen all at once
when we first place our faith in God. It happens over time as the Holy
Spirit works in our lives. That is why the Bible sometimes refers to
salvation as a process rather than just an event.

In Philippians 2:12–13, Paul says:

> Therefore, my dear friends, as you have always obeyed—not only in
> my presence, but now much more in my absence—continue to work
> out your salvation with fear and trembling, for it is God who works in
> you to will and to act according to his good purpose.

Notice how he says, "work *out* your salvation." He did not say we
work *for* our salvation. We already have it. But it is something that
continues to grow. Then he assures us that God is at work to change us.

It is important to understand that much of the language about
salvation refers to this process rather than to the initial event of turning
to God. If you don't understand this distinction, the Bible can be very
confusing. For example, in Galatians 5:24, Paul says that God has
done away with our sinful nature,

> Those who belong to Christ have crucified their sinful nature along
> with its passions and desires.

This can be a startling statement, especially if you are a Christian
and have experienced sinful desires! But we should realize this kind
of language is not unusual when the Bible talks about salvation.

Sometimes the Bible speaks of the whole process as an accomplished fact, when really it is a process that is still going on. Paul is fully aware of this process and teaches it repeatedly. Earlier in the same chapter of Galatians, he refers to the presence and activity of our "sinful desires."

> For the sinful nature desires what is contrary to the Spirit, and the Spirit what is contrary to the sinful nature. They are in conflict with each other, so that you do not do what you want (Gal. 5:17).

(Sometimes Christians make the mistake of thinking everything has changed. This kind of thinking can be very harmful. We'll discuss it in the next chapter.)

How do I know that I have been saved?

Finally, we need to spend a little time on the issue of "assurance." Assurance is the biblical teaching that our salvation is secure and that we can be confident of our security. To put it another way, once we are forgiven we are always forgiven. Yet Christians constantly wonder about this, especially when they sin big. There are two ways we can look at assurance: as an objective fact and as a subjective experience.

Assurance as an objective fact

By "objective fact" I mean something we know from the Scriptures, so we place our faith in it. For example, if I believe the Bible to be God's Word, then it tells me that he loves me and cares for me (1 John 4:10; Luke 11:5–7). That is a truth I put my faith in. Then there is the experience of God's love. Sometimes I feel like God loves me, sometimes I don't.

It's the same way with the assurance of our salvation. Scripture teaches that once God forgives us, he will never judge us. Some we have already covered, like John 5:24 or Hebrews 10:14. I think Hebrews 10:14 is good to look at again because it is so strong and sweeping in its terminology.

> By one sacrifice he [Jesus Christ] has made perfect forever those who are being made holy.

Here the key words are "made perfect" and "forever." One who has turned to God in faith (i.e., "one who is holy," translated as "saint" in other versions) is forever blameless. No matter what we do or don't do, we are perfect. Other scriptures specifically refer to the faithfulness of God's love for those who are his.

> My sheep listen to my voice; I know them, and they follow me. I give them eternal life, and they shall never perish; no one can snatch them out of my hand.
> My Father, who has given them to me, is greater than all; no one can snatch them out of my Father's hand (John 10:27–29).

One of the strongest passages on this topic is in Romans 8:38–39:

> For I am convinced that neither death nor life, neither angels nor demons, neither the present nor the future, nor any powers, neither height nor depth, nor anything else in all creation, will be able to separate us from the love of God that is in Christ Jesus our Lord.

What can separate us from God's love? Nothing! is the resounding answer. This is something to put our faith in whether we feel like it or not. God's love is so unconditional there is nothing we can do to turn him away.

Assurance as a subjective experience

On the other hand, we all want to know subjectively, on an experiential level, that our salvation is secure. We want to know we really are Christians, destined for heaven. In fact, at one point, Paul urged the Corinthians, "examine yourselves to see whether you are in the faith" (2 Cor. 13:5). He was talking about the idea of confirming whether or not they were really Christians.

How essential it is to simply believe God is faithful! Sometimes it is hard. But that is faith—to keep trusting God about something he has promised even when it doesn't seem likely. On the other hand, I also believe it is legitimate to want more experiential knowledge of your relationship with God. Peter gives us some insight on how we may do this in 2 Peter 1:4–10:

> He has given us his very great and precious promises, so that through them you may participate in the divine nature and escape the corruption in the world caused by evil desires.
> For this very reason, make every effort to add to your faith goodness; and to goodness, knowledge; and to knowledge, self-control; and to self-control, perseverance; and to perseverance, godliness; and to godliness, brotherly kindness; and to brotherly kindness, love. For if

you possess these qualities in increasing measure, they will keep you from being ineffective and unproductive in your knowledge of our Lord Jesus Christ. But if anyone does not have them, he is nearsighted and blind, and has forgotten that he has been cleansed from his past sins.

Therefore, my brothers, be all the more eager to make your calling and election sure. For if you do these things, you will never fall.

Here is a list of things that characterize the Christian lifestyle. Things like kindness, self-control, and love are the things God wants to accomplish in our lives. Notice especially verse 10 where Peter says that we ought to be "eager to make our calling and election sure." In other words, we ought to seek to know, experientially, that we are born again. He concludes, "If we are doing these things then we will never fall." It is by living a godly lifestyle that we see God at work in our lives. We see him change us. We see his power and his love at work and it removes any doubt about whether we are his.

I see this truth at work all the time. When I'm submitting to God and letting him have his way with me then I know he lives inside me and is changing me. I see it every day! But when I'm resistant and I'm not sure I want his way in my life, then our relationship can get cold and distant. I don't enjoy the *experience* of assurance.

Think about a time when you really knew God was at work in your life. I'll bet it looked somewhat like Peter's description, learning things, getting closer to people, and working on your relationship with God.

Study summary

Key Points

- Even though Jesus died for all sins, not everyone is forgiven by God. The reason some receive God's forgiveness and not others is faith. A heart of faith is necessary to have Christ's death count for us.
- Many words in the Bible describe the response of faith towards God, including receive, ask, seek, turn (repent), and confess.
- Even though salvation is a free gift available to anyone who believes, most people will not respond to this good news. The reason is that the message of the cross is an offense to our pride. It says we can do nothing to earn God's acceptance. All our religion, efforts, and goodness amount to nothing when it comes to God's forgiveness.
- "Grace" is the term used to describe God's absolutely free offer

of salvation. It is contrasted with "works" or "law" in the Bible, which represent the usual religious approaches to gain God's favor.

- When we turn to God in faith, the Bible describes the transition as justification. We are also given the Holy Spirit, who comes to live inside us. We are given the gift of eternal life. The transition is also described as being born again, made new, and saved.
- Salvation is also a process that continues throughout our life on earth. This is the process of spiritual growth. Once we receive God's forgiveness there is nothing we can do to lose it. We are eternally secure in his love for us.
- We may also have the *experience* of knowing that God loves us if we follow him and draw near to him. It is possible to live in such a way that we are relationally distant from God, so we don't experience the assurance of his love.

Key Scriptures
- John 3:16–18
- John 5:24
- John 1:12
- Luke 11:11–13
- Ezekiel 18:32
- Romans 10:9–10
- Ephesians 2:8–9
- Romans 3:24
- Galatians 2:21
- Romans 5:1
- Romans 8:16
- Titus 3:3–6
- Romans 8:38–39

Important Terms
- Faith / Belief
  Entrusting yourself to God's love and goodness. In the case of salvation, this means believing that God is so loving, he gave his life for us. It means turning to God and believing that his death covers my sins.

- Receive
  Asking for Christ's work to apply to you. When we receive Christ, we are inviting him to apply the work of the cross to us. We are believing that his death pays for our sins.

- Ask / Seek
  In prayer, to call out to the Lord with an attitude of humility. To seek the Lord is to admit we need him. When we ask, he gives us his forgiveness and his Holy Spirit.

- Turn
  To change your perspective and approach God with humility. Since we are all proud and independent, turning to God always involves a decision to change our attitude and perspective. Sometimes called "repentance," this is the change of mind we go through at salvation and whenever we resolve a conflict with God.

- Confess
  To agree with God. We can confess our sins, which means to agree with God that something was sinful. We can confess the truth, which means to agree with God that he speaks the truth. "Confessing Christ" means to agree with God that we need Christ's forgiveness. "Confessing Christ as Lord" means to agree with God that he is our rightful authority.

- Grace
  God's active love towards us. When God forgives us, it is because of his grace. When God works through us, it is because of his grace. When God's love moves out to do something for us, that is grace.

- Law
  The standards God gave in the Old Testament. The Law of Moses was a group of hundreds of moral, civil, and ceremonial prescriptions in the Old Testament.

  Can describe an approach we take in our relationship with God. We can come to God on the basis of his grace or on the basis of law. If we approach God on the basis of law, we would be asking him to accept us because we lived up to some set of rules or code of behavior.

- Justification
  When God views us as innocent. Based on Christ's death for us, when we turn to God in faith he views us as sinless, innocent. Justification refers to how God views us, not our behavior.

- Eternal life
  Being reunited with God. Death is separation from God; the gift of life is coming back into a relationship with him. Eternal life begins now and will culminate in a perfect relationship with God in heaven.

- Born again
  The miraculous transition from death to life, from sin to justification. Because salvation is so revolutionary, it is described by the metaphor of being born again—something no human could ever hope to accomplish on his own.

- Made alive / Made new
  Speaks of the way God views us as innocent and the resulting new relationship we have with him. Because we are forgiven, we are reunited with God. That is new life. Because he views us as innocent, it is as if we are new creations.

- Salvation
  The deliverance we experience because we believe in Christ's death for us. Salvation implies judgment. We are saved from an inevitable doom because of Christ.

  The process of deliverance from the effects of sin. Even though we are immediately delivered from the judgment we deserve, the effects of sin will cling to us for a lifetime. This is why salvation sometimes refers to the lifelong process of spiritual growth.

- Assurance
  The promises God gives us in the Bible that he will never reject us. We can place our faith in God's faithfulness and unconditional love. We can be assured of our future in heaven.

  The inner experience of our relationship with God. The more we follow God and allow him to change us, the more we will experience his unfailing love. If we do not follow God obediently, then we have the Scriptures which assure us of his love although we may not feel or see God's love at work in our lives.

For Further Reading
- *The Grace of God* by Charles Ryrie, Moody Press, 1963
- *Grace* by Lewis Sperry Chafer, Kregel Publications, 1995
- *Eternal Security* by Charles Stanley, Oliver-Nelson, 1990

CHAPTER SIX

SPIRITUAL GROWTH

The topic of spiritual growth is usually found in books like this under the term "sanctification." I have no problem with this term except that many people do not understand it. So in teaching I always find myself explaining that sanctification means being "set apart by God for his purpose." It means becoming more like Christ and expressing more godly character traits. It's easier to use a term people seem to relate to naturally, like "spiritual growth."

Spiritual growth is the process of change God takes us through after becoming Christians. There are a number of terms used in the Bible to describe growth. Terms like "renew" (Col. 3:10), "transform" (2 Cor. 3:18), and "grow" (2 Peter 3:18) all refer to this concept. Surprisingly, the term we get "sanctify" from is most often used to describe something other than spiritual growth. It is the Greek word *hagios* in its various forms, and is most often used to describe how God views us rather than how God is going to change us. Here is an important distinction— between how God views us and how God wants to change us—and we are going to spend some time discussing it.

How God views us versus how God wants to change us

When we turn to God in faith, he forgives us. Earlier we used the term "justification" to describe our standing before God. It is a courtroom term that means we are innocent. God so completely forgives us that he views us as innocent. There is no better scripture than 2 Corinthians 5:17 to describe how God looks at us:

> Therefore, if anyone is in Christ, he is a new creation; the old has gone, the new has come!

81

No matter what anyone might say about me, God looks at me and sees nothing wrong. That is how absolute his forgiveness is. But am I *actually* innocent? Not at all! The miracle of justification is based on God's choice to forgive me, not on what I do. There remains the issue of what I actually am in day-to-day life—a sinful person with all kinds of flaws. This is where spiritual growth comes in. God wants to change us in our day-to-day experience; to gradually turn us into the type of person he already sees.

Justification is accomplished once and for all when we first become Christians. The process of spiritual growth is constantly changing as God deals with issues in our lives. I have borrowed the following chart from Richard Prior's book, *The Way of Holiness*.[1]

Justification	Sanctification
1. Concerns guilt	1. Concerns pollution
2. Legal, external	2. Experiential, internal
3. Relates to our position	3. Relates to our condition
4. Righteousness imputed	4. Righteousness imparted
5. Has no degrees (a person is either "guilty" or not)	5. Has degrees (some have progressed further than others)
6. Once-for-all, not repeated	6. A gradual process
7. By declaration of God	7. By operation of the Spirit
8. No place for works	8. Our cooperation by exercise of the will required.

What actually changes when I am justified?

Justification is an act of God to declare me innocent. But I think everyone wonders what actually changes inside me when God justifies me? God declares me innocent but am I any different than I was before I ever heard of the cross? There are some different answers on this subject, and I think it's an important enough question that we should spend some time on it.

One point of view teaches that virtually everything about us radically changes at the moment of salvation. When we are justified, we are transformed through and through by the power of God's Spirit. One author who teaches on this topic explains:

---

1. Richard Prior, *The Way of Holiness* (Downers Grove, Ill.: InterVarsity, 1982), p. 67

Your old sinful self was destroyed forever. You were made a partaker of the divine nature, the nature of Christ. You became a new person in Christ and you were declared by God to be a saint. This was a one-time transformation. There is nothing you can do to improve upon God's activity in transforming you and justifying you (Neil Anderson, *Victory Over Darkness*, p. 84–85).

Notice the link between the terms "transformation" and "justification." The author is saying justification also involves a transformation of our nature. This means our desires change, the things that make us happy change, we gain new power.

Another author, David Needham, talks about the real change that occurs in a Christian the moment they are justified.

I am a person who in terms of my most essential nature (deepest self, inner man, new man) is a creation of God who does not sin. I am righteous—by nature delighting in the law of God. This new man is not simply a capacity; it is the real me. The person I once was (the old man) I am no more. I am not by nature a 'child of wrath' anymore. I am a child of light. If I died right now, I would be fit for heaven. And heaven is not a place for people who go against their natural tendencies to do what is right. It is a place for those who *by nature* do what is right! (emphasis his). [2]

This is a good example of the point of view we are discussing. Something has really changed within this Christian because of justification. Now they want to follow God. Now they hate sin. Their desires, drives, feelings, and thoughts have been altered by God.

Some Scriptures seem to agree with the idea that we totally change at the moment of salvation. For example, the notion of being "born again," found in several verses in the Bible (John 3:3; Titus 3:5; 1 Peter 1:23), seems to speak of some radical transformation of our character. Romans 6:1–11, probably the most discussed passage on this topic, indicates a new character or nature at the time of our salvation.

However, there are frequent misunderstandings of both the term "born again" and Romans 6. Jesus used the term "born again" in his conversation with the religious leader Nicodemus (John 3:1). He told Nicodemus that he cannot see the kingdom of God unless he is born

---

2. Needham, D. *Birthright: Christian, Do You Know Who You Are?* (Portland, Ore.: Multnomah Press, 1978), 78.

again. Remember that this had an unsettling effect on Nicodemus. He replied, "How can a man be born when he is old? He can't enter a second time into his mother's womb and be born, can he?" Here is the key to understanding Jesus' use of the term—it rattled Nicodemus. Jesus' aim was to shake the confidence of this renowned religious leader. That is why he went on to say to Nicodemus:

> "You are Israel's teacher," said Jesus, "and do you not understand these things? . . . I have spoken to you of earthly things and you do not believe; how then will you believe if I speak of heavenly things? (John 3:10–12).

Jesus wanted Nicodemus to come to the point where he said, "I don't understand." Only then could he really hear what Jesus was saying because Nicodemus thought he knew it all. Jesus used the "born again" metaphor to force Nicodemus to take the seat of the learner. The metaphor was meant to teach that God had to work a miracle—something Nicodemus was incapable of. Jesus went on to describe the notion of forgiveness with the famous verses of John 3:16–17.

Being "born again" means God works a miracle no less amazing than a physical rebirth—forgiveness at the expense of Jesus Christ. It does not necessarily imply that we are wholly changed at the moment of forgiveness. There is a danger in taking metaphors like "born again" and making them say things they were never intended to say.

In Romans 6, Paul addresses the issue of sinning Christians. He opens the chapter up with the question, "What shall we say, then? Shall we go on sinning so that grace may increase?" Many a Christian has asked something similar to this. If God's forgiveness is complete even for sins I'll commit in the future, then why not taste the fruit of sin for a while? Paul's answer has caused a lot of furrowed brows and crinkled noses, "By no means! We died to sin; how can we live in it any longer?"

Just how did we die to sin? Does it mean we don't want to sin anymore? Does it mean there is no drive for sin in our lives? These are tough questions. And I know the answers we arrive at will have big implications for our lives.

First, let's consider the statement, "We have died to sin." Paul speaks as if something is already completely accomplished. Yet just two chapters later in Romans 8:13, Paul speaks of our relationship to sin as an *ongoing process* of death. "If by the Spirit you are putting to death the deeds of the body you will live" (taking "deeds of the body" as synonymous with sin). In other words, in one passage he says we died to sin as an accomplished fact. But just a short time later he says we must put sin to death. I know Paul is not so forgetful or confused that he would contradict himself in such a short space. This is just like the passage in Galatians 5 we discussed earlier. Paul is talking about two different ideas here.

In Romans 6:2, Paul wrote, "God views us as having died to sin." He was referring to justification. Why should God's view of us make us want to quit sinning? Let's keep reading:

> Or don't you know that all of us who were baptized into Christ Jesus were baptized into his death? We were therefore buried with him through baptism into death in order that, just as Christ was raised from the dead through the glory of the Father, we too may live a new life (Rom. 6:3–4).

This language of "baptism" in verse 3 is a Christian term to refer to our salvation, since baptism and salvation were always hand-in-hand. He is saying that when we were saved we were identified with Jesus Christ's death for us. Again, this has to do with how God views us. He views us as having died with Christ. We have even been buried with him! That is why he so completely forgives us.

Paul goes on to say that just as Christ was raised from the dead, we also have been raised to "live a new life." Here is why God's view of us is so influential. Now that he sees us as forgiven, he accepts us, loves us, and takes up a relationship with us. "Life" in the Bible is synonymous with God. God is the source of life. To be in fellowship with God is to have life. To be cut off from God is death. That's why God promised Adam and Eve that the day they ate of the fruit, they would surely die! That day they were cut off from their Creator.

Now we can "walk in new life," as some translations render verse 4. Now we have fellowship with God again. This is no small change! God sends his Holy Spirit to live in us, change us, and empower us. Paul devotes much of Romans 8 to discussing this. But the question before us now is, "Does that mean *I* change when God forgives me?" At the very moment he sends his Holy Spirit to live in me, is there anything *else* new and different about me? Romans 6 is only saying that God views me differently. Because of that, I can now have fellowship with him.

There are two more points about Romans 6 that are often misunderstood. As Paul goes on in the chapter, he continues to say some powerful things about how God views us. Let's look further.

> If we have been united with him like this in his death, we will certainly also be united with him in his resurrection (Rom. 6:5).

This verse repeats the notion that God sees us as joined to Christ in all his sufferings and his resurrection. Then Paul makes some statements that have become very controversial.

> For we know that our old self was crucified with him so that the body of sin might be done away with, that we should no longer be slaves to sin (Rom. 6:6).

Paul is really getting at the question he started with, "Should I continue in sin because of God's grace?" Paul answers this by saying, "Now that you have been totally forgiven, you have a choice! You don't have to sin all the time because there is an alternative!" The way he says this is by referring back to these very colorful images, "Your old self was crucified! Your body of sin has been done away with!"

Now if you read and understand the first part of this chapter, then you understand that Paul is saying God *views* us as having been crucified. God *views* our sinful body as having been put to death. His perspective should begin to effect the way we look at ourselves. My fourth grade teacher, Mrs. Basil, thought for some reason that I was one of the best students in the class. This was a real contrast to all my previous teachers, who thought that I was the best trouble-maker in the class. Mrs. Basil's view of me had a profound affect, however, because for that year I *was* one of the best students in the class. If God loves us, has a high view of us, and sees all kinds of potential that should affect the way we view ourselves. His opinion of us, after all, is ultimately the only one that matters.

So God's view of us makes a relationship with him possible, and it should affect the way we look at ourselves. In actual practice, we are still the same person. We still struggle with sin. Our bodies and minds still crave the same things. But Paul says because we have been forgiven and united with God, there is a way out. There is a choice now.

Of course, Paul is assuming we have a desire for freedom from sin. The picture he paints is that of a prisoner whose chains have been broken and whose prison door is open. It is up to us to walk through that door now to real, experiential freedom.

To emphasize his point, he repeats in verse 7:

Because anyone who has died has been justified from sin.

The problem is that most translations render the term "justified" as "freed." The term is the Greek word, *dikaioō*. When Paul uses it elsewhere he is referring to our forgiveness. We studied it previously when discussing salvation. It is a legal term, describing our standing before God. We are innocent.

Translating the term as "freed from sin" is misleading because it can give the impression that we will no longer struggle with sin. That is definitely not true. The next two chapters of Romans are dedicated to discussing the prolonged and fierce battle with sin in the life of a Christian. Being justified from sin *does* mean that we now have the freedom to turn to God for power and victory over our sins. Before, we were alienated from the life of God. Now we have him living inside us.

The struggle runs deep

Scripture tell us that the struggle against sin in our lives is fierce, prolonged, and very deep. In Galatians 5:17, Paul describes sanctification in terms of a battle.

For the sinful nature desires what is contrary to the Spirit, and the Spirit what is contrary to the sinful nature. They are in conflict with each other, so that you do not do what you want.

God's Spirit is at work within us. He cultivates within us a desire to follow God. Just how strong and how quickly that desire develops is different from Christian to Christian. The point is this godly desire is at odds with our sinful nature (*flesh* in other translations), which is still very strong within us.

The way Paul summarizes this struggle is interesting. He says, "So that you don't do what you want." Debate rages on which side is not getting what it wants, the sinful nature or the Spirit? But Paul says neither! It's *you* who doesn't get what *you* want! The problem is that you, the real you, wants both. When I submit to the Spirit, my sinful nature is not gratified. When I submit to the flesh, the Spirit is grieved and I feel the grief with him.

It's true that the Christian life can be frustrating. But don't let that take away from the fact that as we let the Spirit change us, there is a growing sense of joy, wholeness, and love in our lives. Just read on in Galatians as Paul describes the "fruit of the Spirit"—the things God will produce in our lives if we let him.

> But the fruit of the Spirit is love, joy, peace, patience, kindness, goodness, faithfulness, gentleness and self-control. Against such things there is no law (Gal. 5:22–23).

Paul doesn't feed people the illusion that somehow they will have very little struggle against sin now that they have been born again. He is straight up: "You will be very frustrated." Nevertheless, the rewards of letting God have his way are far greater than the fleeting pleasures of continuing in sin.

This brings me to an issue that greatly concerns me. I have seen so many Christians hurt and disillusioned because they were fed inflated expectations. They were told that now that they are new creatures, they should have complete victory over sin! Now that they are Christians, they won't even want to sin anymore! For support, people turn to Romans 6, especially verses 6 and 7, "We are no longer slaves to sin, for the one who has died has been freed from sin." There are some serious dangers in exaggerating the actual change that occurs when God forgives us.

The dangers of exaggeration
Failure to appreciate the struggle

When people are taught that their entire nature and character changes at salvation, they can't help having a shallow view of the struggle against sin. Sin runs deep. As we discussed in our chapter on sin, it's not just some behavioral problem or breaking rules. Sin is rooted in our character—the proud desire to run our own lives.

Then some people come along and teach that our desires have completely changed. They say that our character has changed. So how do they explain the continued struggle with sin? For many, they explain the battle as nothing more than a matter of training bodily urges and habits. They make a distinction between the "old self" of Romans 6:6 and the "body of sin." The real you was completely overhauled at salvation but you still have the "body of sin." This, they teach, was only "rendered powerless."

> For we know that our old self was crucified with him so that the body of sin might be *rendered powerless* (instead of "done away with"), that we should no longer be slaves to sin.

Interestingly, those who make this distinction between the "body of sin" and our "sinful nature" say our problem is that we are still confined to this physical body. [3] Our body has been trained to enjoy sinful urges. Our body has deeply ingrained habits. One author puts it this way:

> What then does the term "the body of sin" mean? It means the body, our physical body, of which sin has taken possession . . . Here is the vital distinction as I see it, the distinction between "I myself as a personality" and "my body."
> Sin still remains and is left in our bodies; not in us, but in our bodies. As persons, as souls, we have already finished with it, but not so the body. This body of sin—this body which sin inhabits and tries to use— still remains . . . sin not only remains in our bodies; but if it is not checked, if it is not kept under, it will even reign in our bodies, and it will dominate our bodies. [4]

I really like the teaching and insightful application of Dr. Martin Lloyd-Jones. But this part of his teaching I cannot agree with because it is typical of so many who see the problem of sin as only skin deep.

For example, if a person came to Christ and had a problem with drugs or alcohol, I could tell him his problem is merely a physical addiction. Now that God has revamped the real you, you need to change the physical addiction you have!

I've seen this tried. I know it doesn't work. Fortunately, it's not biblical either. The truth is that using drugs and alcohol is more than a physical urge. Habits like these are related to much deeper problems, like how I view myself, where I get my emotional stimulation from, and whether I really want God's way in my life or not.

So it goes with countless other sins. We could struggle with them at the surface level, pretending they are only the residual habits of our past life, stored in our brain tissue or driven by our glands. And we will fail because we will not come to grips with the real problem—

---

3. I don't want to get more deeply into the study of Romans 6:6 except to say that the most simple and straightforward rendering of the terms Paul used is, "done away with," not, "rendered powerless." See commentators on this passage such as John Murray. *New International Commentary on the N.T.: Epistle to the Romans* (Wm. B. Eerdmans, 1968), 220–221; Anders Nygren. *Commentary on Romans* (Fortress, 1949), 239. See also the translation of the KJV, NASB and RSV.

4. Lloyd-Jones, *Romans, The New Man*, 72, 153

me, all of me. Through and through I love to rebel against God! God still has some serious work to do in changing me.

A *shallow view of sin*

A related danger of exaggerating the change God works at salvation is a shallow view of individual sins. On the one hand, we can fail to appreciate how deep our sinful desires run. On the other hand, we can fail to appreciate the seriousness of particular sins we stumble over.

For example, let's pretend a Christian lusts for a woman from time to time. I have actually witnessed Christians casting out the demon of lust in a situation like this! Their reasoning? "Christians don't lust! If you have a lust problem, then it must be a demon!"

Now I don't doubt for a minute that spirits can and do tempt us with lust. But it is also completely normal for Christians to struggle with this. When we credit it to a demon, it actually trivializes the problem. It makes the problem out to be something I don't really have. So, instead of taking it seriously and looking to God for help and healing, I could just go on thinking the problem isn't there anymore.

Seeing our sin should alert us to the need for God's healing.

Excessive guilt and feelings of rejection from God

Ironically, the teaching that we have been completely changed at salvation, which I'm sure is intended as a very positive message, can turn out to do some real damage. Some Christians have become enslaved to the fear of "backsliding." Since "real Christians" don't want to sin anymore, those who do enjoy sin are either under the influence of a demon or are not really Christians!

Taking the example of lust, imagine a person leaving a prayer session where the "demon" of lust was authoritatively cast out. He goes out into the street and there's a nice-looking girl! He starts to lust. But he just had that demon eradicated! Now what? He can either judge himself, "Oooh, you sinner! You man of little faith!" or he can start making pronouncements at the demon again, "Away from me demon! I already told you to get away!" Or he can even pretend he didn't really lust. It is actually possible to attempt to ignore thoughts and sins like this. It is certainly possible to pretend to others that you have had victory over the problem!

Many Christians aren't able to live up to the charade. So they finally conclude that they must be terrible Christians. They must have no faith because they keep stumbling. Or worse yet, maybe they weren't even Christians in the first place. Often, Christians who call themselves "backslidden Christians" mean something like this.

An avoidance orientation

If my new nature is essentially on the right track in harmony with God's will, then the only real danger comes from letting my body have its way or listening to the seductive voices of the world around me. This is the reasoning that drives many Christians to develop an *avoidance orientation.* I have to avoid letting my body rule. I have to avoid the demons. I have to avoid the world. If I can effectively avoid these things, then I can have victory over sin.

Since my new nature is pretty much in touch with God, it'll just cruise along. What we have to worry about is letting the flesh get its way or the demons get their way or the world suggest its way.

If we realize, however, that we are still just as proud and just as rebellious against God as ever, then we'll see that mere avoidance means nothing. You could deny your body, deny the world, deny Satan, and still be completely in sin. Because sin is me, doing *my* thing. Sin is my pride. Sin is my autonomy. If we realize this, then we should be much more concerned with the positive direction—going out of my way to find ways to serve God. I'm not in perfect submission to him. I have to consciously go out of my way to turn myself over to God. It isn't natural.

I remember a story from a missionary that reminds me of similar things I have seen. A girl in one of his churches was campaigning to have women cover their arms fully because bare arms were worldly. The issue caused quite a controversy in their church as people debated whether they should mandate covered arms. Well, the woman who began the controversy kept her arms covered for the most part, except when she was having an affair with the pastor of the church!

The real sadness of stories like this is that they are so common. Christians underestimate the reality of their own sin. They get caught up in avoiding some external representation of sin, only to be ruined when the real thing overtakes them from within.

Conclusion: There are no easy answers

So we've seen that when God saves us, he views us as perfect. He views us as having died and risen again to a new life. As a result, he comes to have fellowship with us. The Holy Spirit comes to live with us to change us. But there is a lot to change. God's view of us is *in spite of the reality* that we have big, big problems. We saw that God's view of us is important because it enables us to have fellowship with him. When we have fellowship with God, he changes us. The way he views us doesn't mean he *has changed* us. That will come. That is the process of sanctification.

We also saw that there are dangers to exaggerating our actual change at conversion. We could imagine a cancer patient who prays for healing with other Christians. Someone prophesies, "Yes, God has granted our request!" So the cancer patient goes away, joyous at God's healing power. What would happen, though, if the patient turns up a year later with advanced cancer? Now it's too late! Imagine the guilt, the doubt, the anger! I've seen Christians go through something like this when they find out their sinful nature is still as strong as ever.

No doubt, there will be Christians who disagree with me about the extent of change at the moment of conversion. I believe the Bible leaves room for a range of views on this topic. So often it describes our sanctification in terms of tension and dichotomies. We are both "fleshly" and "not fleshly" (see Rom. 7:17–18; Gal. 5:24). We are pure, yet we need purifying (see 1 John 3:3). All things are new, yet we are being renewed (see 2 Cor. 5:17; Col. 3:10).

If God had described spiritual growth to us in tidy, clear categories, we would turn it into a legalistic heresy. We would love to say, "Just take step A, then B, then C . . . and then pick up your diploma." Instead, God has communicated the path of progress to us in dichotomies and tensions. The result should be that we rely on him all the more to show us the way. We'll turn now to the issue of what spiritual growth is and how to pursue it.

Study summary

Key Points
- Justification speaks of the way God looks at us, whereas spiritual growth (sanctification) is the process of change we go through after we are justified. Even though God may view us as faultless (justified), we are not actually without sin. Spiritual growth is the process of becoming more like the way God views us.
- The main change that takes place at salvation is the Holy Spirit coming to live within us. Beyond that, it is not clear that our old nature changes right away. We should beware that the tendency toward sin is just as present as ever.
- The dangers of exaggerating the changes which take place when we are first saved include: a failure to appreciate the struggle against sin; a shallow view of sin; excessive guilt and feelings of rejection from God; and an avoidance orientation.
- Spiritual growth is often portrayed in the Bible in terms of

tensions and dichotomies. There is no quick and easy system for spiritual maturity.

Key Scriptures
- 2 Corinthians 5:17
- Romans 6:1–14
- Galatians 5:17–24

Important Terms
- Spiritual growth
  The process of change God effects in our lives. Our entire lives here on earth will be a process of growth in spiritual maturity.

- Sanctification
  The process of change God effects in our lives. Sanctification is also a term used to describe spiritual growth.

  Our status as "set apart" in God's eyes. Sometimes "sanctification" and "sanctified" refer to the way God views us. The words mean to be "set apart." In the Bible, the word "holy" is sometimes used for the same idea.

- Old self
  Our life before meeting Christ. Everything we were and did is viewed as the "old self." It is also possible to revert to the ways of the "old self" by living the way we did before Christ.

For Further Reading
- *Christian Spirituality: Five Views of Sanctification* edited by Donald Alexander, InterVarsity, 1988
- *Five Views On Sanctification* by Melvin Dieter, Zondervan, 1987
- *The Pursuit of Holiness* by Jerry Bridges, NavPress, 1978
- *The Normal Christian Life* by Watchman Nee, Tyndale, 1983
- *Spiritual Maturity* by J. Oswald Sanders, Moody Press, 1962

CHAPTER SEVEN

SPIRITUAL GROWTH: GETTING CLOSE TO GOD

A relational goal

There are so many goals we could set for spiritual growth. We could say growing spiritually means sinning less. We could then define which sins should go first. We might define spiritual growth as becoming more spiritually powerful—power for God's service, power for a successful Christian life. We could define spiritual growth as separation from the world. All of these goals can be found and defended in the Scriptures.

There is, however, an over-arching goal for spiritual growth. It is a theme that runs from beginning to end in the Bible. It is a goal that defines all other goals. It is the goal of getting to know God. It is a relational goal. Growing in your relationship with God defines how far you are in spiritual growth.

Scriptures which teach a relational goal

In Ephesians 4, Paul says the goal of the church's work is to help people grow to maturity.

> . . . until we all reach unity in the faith and in the knowledge of the Son of God and become mature, attaining to the whole measure of the fullness of Christ (Eph. 4:13).

Paul uses several phrases to describe spiritual growth here: "the unity of the faith," "knowledge of the Son of God," and "mature." The goal of knowing God is clear in the second phrase, "knowledge of the Son of God." As Paul goes on, he makes this goal paramount.

> Then we will no longer be infants, tossed back and forth by the waves, and blown here and there by every wind of teaching and by the cunning and craftiness of men in their deceitful scheming. Instead, speaking the truth in love, we will in all things grow up into him who is the Head, that is, Christ (vv. 14–15).

Instead of being infants (spiritually immature), we are to grow up. One of the side-effects of maturity will be stability and discernment. Notice carefully that growing up is "into him." We are to grow closer and closer to Christ. That's maturity.

In Philippians 3, Paul talks about his goals as a Christian.

> What is more, I consider everything a loss compared to the surpassing greatness of knowing Christ Jesus my Lord, for whose sake I have lost all things. I consider them rubbish, that I may gain Christ (Phil. 3:8).

Paul says that knowing Christ is the greatest thing he has ever had. He concludes this verse by saying his goal is to gain more of Christ. He continues in verse 9:

> And be found in him, not having a righteousness of my own that comes from the law, but that which is through faith in Christ—the righteousness that comes from God and is by faith. I want to know Christ and the power of his resurrection and the fellowship of sharing in his sufferings, becoming like him in his death.

On the one hand, Paul says that he knows Christ. Yet he wants to know more of Christ. He repeats this longing in different ways. This is the goal that keeps Paul going.

The biblical imagery of "walking with God" also speaks of a growing personal relationship. In the New Testament, the phrase "walking with God" or "walking by the Spirit" describes spiritual growth (Rom. 8:4–5; Gal. 5:16). In the Old Testament, godly men and women "walked with God." Enoch walked with God so closely that God took him home to heaven (Gen. 5:24).

Moses longed for a closer relationship with God. In Exodus 33:13, he asked God:

> Now, then, I beg of you, if I have found favor in your sight, let me
> know your ways, so that I can know you, so that I may privileged in
> your sight.

Later Moses asked to see God. God told him that if he saw him
face to face, Moses would die. He did allow Moses to see the after-
effects of his passing by. But here was the desire I'm talking about—
the desire to know God more closely.

David was unique in his desire to know God. It's impossible to
read his psalms and not see how much he longed to be close to God
(see Psalms 25:4–5; 73:25, 28). God himself describes David as "a
man after my own heart" (1 Sam. 13:14).

In the Old Testament, there are verses that promise blessing to
those who "wait upon the Lord" (Isa. 30:14; 40:31). But "waiting" is
not such a good translation of the term. Waiting is when you sit in the
rocker and wait for the cows to come home. It is more accurate to
translate the term as "longing." God is saying that we are spiritually
blessed and rewarded when we long for him.

I could go on with other passages. Many of the terms and images we
commonly use to refer to spiritual growth reflect God's desire to have
a relationship with us. When God calls on us to be "holy," it's not just
a lifestyle or a change of habits. The call to holiness is a call to closeness.
To be "holy" means to be "separate." The call to be separate was given
to the Old Testament believers in the context of a promise, "I will dwell
with them and walk among them. I will be their God and they shall be
my people" (Ex. 29:45; Lev. 26:12). He doesn't just want us separate
for the sake of being different. He is saying, "Come closer to me. I
want to be with you!"

Paul interprets God's call to holiness as a call to a closer relationship
with him.

> "I will dwell in them and walk among them; and I will be their God,
> and they shall be My people. Therefore, come out from their midst
> and be separate," says the Lord. "And do not touch what is unclean;
> And I will welcome you. And I will be a father to you, And you shall
> be sons and daughters to Me," says the Lord Almighty
> (2 Corinthians 6:16b–18 NASB).

Do you see how Paul unites the idea of holiness (being separate)
with the idea of closeness with God? That's why God calls us out!
"Come over here! I want to be your father, and you can be my sons
and daughters!"

If Christians realized that this is what God really wanted, they would be more excited about spiritual growth. I have sometimes had the impression that spiritual growth is a matter of quitting fun things and disciplining myself to like things that are boring—not a very appealing picture. But when I realized God wants to know me, I had to have it! The notion of getting close to God is exciting.

The means God gives us

Let's talk about some avenues God has given us to draw nearer to him.

The Bible

First, there is the Bible. Some people think this book is boring. Sadly, it has often been taught to us in a boring way, so there is good reason for some people to believe it is boring.

But to anyone who thinks this, I have a challenge. Open it up with a friend and read a paragraph. Read out of the gospels (the first four books of the New Testament). Or read out of one of Paul's letters (e.g. Philippians, Colossians). Then stop and ask each other, "What do you think it means?" Just bat it back and forth. Get a few people involved. Then go further and ask, "What do you think God is trying to tell us through this?"

If you do this, you will see that this book speaks. It's alive. God actually speaks to us as we read its pages. Hebrews 4:12 says:

> For the word of God is living and active. Sharper than any double-edged sword, it penetrates even to dividing soul and spirit, joints and marrow; it judges the thoughts and attitudes of the heart.

That's what I'm talking about! It pierces. It exposes. God's Word speaks to us. I get upset when a preacher or Bible teacher gets up and talks about God's Word in a disinterested, ho-hum way, "Blah, blah, blah . . ." He's not communicating it for what it really is—the living Word of God!

Peter, in his first letter, writes:

> Like newborn babes, long for the pure milk of the word, that by it you may grow in respect to salvation (1 Peter 2:2 NASB).

Long for it! That should be our attitude. This verse is especially good because it shows us that spiritual growth is only possible if we have the food God provides, his Word. Lots of people think they are going to grow spiritually without really getting into the Scriptures. No way. Spiritual growth is inseparable from the knowledge of the Scriptures (see Heb. 5:12–14).

I want to be very clear that the Scriptures are a tool we use to get close to God. He wants to communicate intimately and personally to us by using the written word. A lot of Christians have never had God speak to them. How grievous when God is just an impersonal abstraction!

There is a story in 1 Samuel 3 that illustrates what happens to a person who is a stranger to God's Word. It starts with a description that could match the lives of many Christians:

> Now the boy Samuel was ministering to the Lord before Eli. And word from the Lord was rare in those days, visions were infrequent (1 Sam. 3:1 NASB).

Word from God was rare in those days. That's the scenario I'm talking about. Samuel was a young man who was learning to be a priest while Eli was the current priest. The story continues to set the stage:

> And it happened at that time as Eli was lying down in his place (now his eyesight had begun to grow dim and he could not see well), and the lamp of God had not yet gone out, and Samuel was lying down in the temple of the Lord where the ark of God was (vv. 2–3).

Eli was getting old and losing his eyesight, so he used to sleep right there in the temple. The lamp was supposed to burn all night. By saying it had not gone out is telling us that it is very late, but not so late that the lamp had already gone out. It is the dead calm of the early morning hours.

> The Lord called Samuel; and he said, "Here I am." Then he ran to Eli and said, "Here I am, for you called me." But he said, "I did not call, lie down again." So he went and lay down (vv. 4–5).

Samuel did what anyone would do. He assumed the voice came from Eli in the next room. So God called to Samuel again.

> And the Lord called yet again, "Samuel!" So Samuel arose and went to Eli, and said, "Here I am, for you called me." But he answered, "I did not call, my son, lie down again" (v. 6).

Surely Samuel suspected something was up. A voice in the middle of the night! And Eli had already said it wasn't him. But again, he went to see if perhaps Eli might be calling him. In the next verse, we learn why Samuel was so hesitant to conclude that he was hearing the voice of God.

> Now Samuel did not yet know the Lord, nor had the word of the Lord yet been revealed to him (v. 7).

It's not that Samuel didn't know about God. He was training to be a priest, after all! What Samuel was missing was the personal knowledge of God that comes from communication. "The word of the Lord had not yet been revealed to him." Here is the point for us to listen to. When the Word of God is rare in our lives, then we don't expect him to speak. The longer we go without hearing from God, the more cynical we become about ever hearing from him. I know. I've experienced months at a stretch where I was just going through the motions; there was no reality to my relationship with God. It got to the point where I thought I was different from other people. They may experience God, but there's something wrong with me.

God finally got through to Samuel, with the help of Eli.

> So the Lord called Samuel again for the third time. And he arose and went to Eli, and said, "Here I am, for you called me." Then Eli discerned that the Lord was calling the boy. And Eli said to Samuel, "Go lie down, and it shall be if he calls you, that you shall say, 'Speak, Lord, for your servant is listening.'" So Samuel went and lay down in his place. Then the Lord came and stood and called as at other times, "Samuel! Samuel!" And Samuel said, "Speak, for your servant is listening." And the Lord said to Samuel, "Behold, I am about to do a thing in Israel at which both ears of everyone who hears it will tingle" (vv. 8–11).

God finally spoke to Samuel fully. Unfortunately, the message God had for Samuel was a sad one. Eli and his sons were going to die. But the point for us to see is that God didn't speak until Samuel recognized who it was and said, "I'm ready to hear from you, Lord." This is the attitude we need before God will speak to us. We must come to the point where we put aside our cynicism and are willing to hear whatever God has to say to us.

When we are ready and willing to hear God's Word, then we must open the Scriptures. This is the means God has chosen to speak. Whether it's by reading the Bible, listening to teaching, studying it with friends, or reading books about the Bible, we must begin to seek a deeper relationship with God in the Scriptures.

Prayer

Along with the written communication of God's Word, we need to speak to God directly through prayer. Prayer is also a time of listening to God. Prayer is simply spending time in open communication with God. In 1 Thessalonians 5:16–18, Paul says we should pray at all times:

> Be joyful always; pray continually; give thanks in all circumstances, for this is God's will for you in Christ Jesus.

This shows that prayer is an attitude of communing and fellowshipping with God that I can enjoy at any time. I don't have to fold my hands or look to the sky. I can be driving my car and thinking my thoughts through *with God.* I can be reflecting on another person *with God.* I can be puzzling through an issue *with God.*

Of course there are times when we want to pray in earnest. At these times we might get alone, keep a prayer list, maybe even get on our knees before God. When you think of it, we set aside times to communicate with our best friends. If we're smart, we make those times special. Then why not do the same thing with God?

The greatest barrier to prayer is our own pride the lack of felt *need* to pray. We may know that it's a good idea to pray, that there are benefits to it, and that we could get closer to God. But if we believe deep-down we can handle things ourselves, then we won't make time for prayer. The Psalmist contrasts two attitudes in Psalms 32:9:

> Do not be like the horse or the mule, which have no understanding but must be controlled by bit and bridle or they will not come to you.

Sometimes we can be like the mule who doesn't understand. He will not come near God unless some hardship or glaring need jerks his head around. The other attitude is that of the person who constantly sees his or her own need and desires closeness with God. This person approaches God willingly and eagerly.

I really struggle with prayer. Sometimes I'll go for a long time without much prayer, and then I wonder why I'm not close to God. God earnestly desires to hear from us. The problem is that we don't feel like we need it. I wish I could tell you just how hard it has been for me to be consistent in my prayer. It is one of the most difficult areas of my spiritual growth. And the amazing thing is, I know it would be good! I know I would enjoy it. I know I would grow closer to God. I know I would get insight in my times of prayer with God. I know all kinds of things about prayer. Yet I don't do it.

That's why I hate stories about people who get up at five o'clock in the morning and pray for three hours. It's like hearing a story about someone who never has a problem with lust or anger. Prayer has been a constant struggle for me and I think it might be that way for a while. I believe that prayer is a struggle for many because we don't *really feel* like we need it. Intellectually we may be able to recite the benefits of prayer. But in our hearts we feel like it would be better to talk to a friend or watch TV than to take time to talk to God.

So, how does God get us to talk to him? The answer should not surprise you: Suffering. Confusion. Hardship. Times when we don't have the answers. These times are the "bit and bridle" that draw us near to God. They break down our pride and show us our need. At these times we think, "Maybe it would be good to spend a lot of time with God." We see this phenomenon in James 1:2–4 (NASB):

> Consider it all joy, my brethren, when you encounter various trials, knowing that the testing of your faith produces endurance. And let endurance have its perfect result, that you may be perfect and complete, lacking in nothing (NASB).

James says that if you are going through hard times, you should rejoice because we know God is at work in hard times! But, haven't you ever wondered, "What in the world is he trying to do? Come on! Tell me God!" James goes on and talks about that feeling of confusion. He suggests we take it to God:

> But if any of you lacks wisdom, let him ask of God, who gives to all men generously and without reproach, and it will be given to him (v. 5).

If you don't understand the hardship you are experiencing, go to God and ask for wisdom. He will give you insight.

One thing I should point out, though, about this promise is that it doesn't tell us when God will give us insight. He will definitely give us wisdom, but maybe not right away. The truth is—and we all hate to hear this—God wants us to be confused at times.

In 2 Corinthians 4:8, Paul lists confusion (perplexity) as a major way God hammers away on our pride. Times of confusion and suffering draw us closer to God. They finally break us down to the point where we say, "OK, maybe I'll go ahead and get some kind of prayer life with God."

Confusion. Suffering. Hardship. I wish there were some other ways God could draw us closer to himself. I wish there were some other ways God could get at our pride and turn us into the kind of people who really feel like we need him. But it seems as if this is the only way a deep prayer life is born.

It's hard for us to understand how a loving God would use suffering to draw us closer to himself. In fact, sometimes when I think of it, I can start to get angry. "Do you mean he was the one behind all those hard times?"

We can start to blame God for the suffering we go through and get a picture of a cruel puppet-master. Let's try to understand suffering a little better by describing three different types.

Suffering from sin

If we were honest with ourselves, we would realize that suffering often comes as a result of our own sin. I have always had a hard time acknowledging this. I remember getting angry at God once because I received several bad grades.

Peter says it is of no value to suffer as an "evildoer" (1 Peter 4:15). He is referring to the principle that Paul cites in Colossians 3:25, "He who does wrong will receive the consequences of that wrong, and that without partiality." Both non-Christians and Christians suffer from their bad decisions. Most of the time, the benefit we receive from such suffering is to learn we shouldn't make that same mistake again.

God's discipline

There is a unique type of suffering, reserved only for God's people, called God's "discipline" in Hebrews 12. Hebrews makes it clear that all Christians are disciplined by God (v. 6). In a sense, God's discipline is also because of our sin. If we had no weakness, we would need no discipline.

But God's discipline is very different from the notion of suffering as a result of particular sins. God's discipline is not punishment of this sin or that sin; it has a broader focus. He is looking at deeper issues in our character and lifestyle. He is trying to shape us. For example, discipline may come in the form of God taking us through a time where we feel very alone or very lost. A period like this may include a sense of confusion, maybe even a feeling of distance from God.

I know some Christians teach it is never God's will for us to experience spiritual "dryness" where we have very little feeling of spiritual victory. But I have already mentioned that Paul sees spiritual confusion as a regular part of his suffering (2 Corinthians 4:8). It is also clear that he experienced times of failure and severe questioning as well (2 Corinthians 7:5). Surely spiritual confusion and failure are due largely to our own sinfulness. That is why we need spiritual growth.

Another form of spiritual discipline may be the people in our lives who confront us. God may use a boss, a spouse, a family member, or a friend to draw attention to a character issue he wants to work on. He may even use demonic adversaries to discipline us (2 Corinthians 12:7). But the main point about God's discipline is that it is positive and forward-looking. God does not want to punish us for particular sins in the past. He is trying to change us. He is applying pressure to draw out a weakness or even cultivate a strength. When we are experiencing God's discipline, the question shouldn't be, "What did I do to deserve this?" It should be, "How is God trying to shape me?" There is something very exciting about the fact that the God of the universe takes time to work on me this way.

Suffering in the course of serving Christ
Finally, there is a type of suffering we can volunteer for! Paul says in Philippians 1:29, "To you it has been granted, for Christ's sake, not only to believe in him, but to suffer for his sake!" In his own life, Paul considered his suffering an honor worth boasting about (2 Cor. 11:23–30). John and Peter also rejoiced in Acts 5 that they were worthy of suffering for Christ.

Why would someone volunteer for extra suffering? Paul explains in several passages that such distress makes us more dependent on God. In 2 Corinthians 1:9, he explains that his own near-death experience made him "trust not in himself, but in the One who can raise us from the dead." You can easily see the connection between suffering and the greater goal of spiritual maturity, the goal of getting closer to God. When we suffer, we draw nearer to God. Without suffering, we are smug, independent, and see no real need for a close and dependent relationship with God.

One of the outcomes of suffering is greater ministry effectiveness. As Paul says in 2 Corinthians 4:12, "Death works in us, but life in you," meaning his suffering resulted in being a more effective conduit for the life of God to the Corinthians.

Other Christians
God also gives us the avenue of involvement with other Christians as a means of getting closer to him. To get close to God's people is to get close to him. We will discuss this when we spend a chapter on the biblical teaching of the church.

Study summary
Key Points
* Spiritual maturity should be understood most basically as deepening our relationship with God. As we get closer to him, we will grow to be more like him.
* A desire to get close to God has been the mark of godly people in the Bible, including Moses, David, and Paul.
* The means God gives us to draw close to him are the Bible, prayer, suffering, and other Christians.

Key Scriptures
* Ephesians 4:11–16
* Philippians 3:8–11
* Hebrews 4:12
* 1 Peter 2:2
* 1 Thessalonians 5:16–18
* Hebrews 12:1–13

Important Terms
* The Bible
  God's word to us, a key to our spiritual growth. Since God actually reveals himself in the Bible, it is one of the main ways we get close to him, which is the goal of spiritual growth.

* Prayer
  Spending time in communication with God. Prayer can be anything from sharing our requests and burdens with God to waiting and listening for his voice. We can think about the issues and people in our life with an attitude of prayer, which means we have a humble, listening heart.

* Suffering
  Going through hard times which draw us closer to God. One of the main motivations for getting closer to God is the fact that we need him and suffering highlights that need. Suffering can be from our own sins, at the hands of other people, or it

can be a lifestyle of pressure, failure, and vulnerability we
volunteer for.

• God's discipline
  Character-oriented training God puts all Christians through.
  Discipline is not punishment for particular sins. It is forward-
  looking and focuses on making us a better person. If God sees
  an issue in our lives that needs attention, sometimes he uses
  circumstances or people, or he simply works in our hearts to
  emphasize the need for change.

For Further Reading
  • *Knowing God* by J. I. Packer, InterVarsity, 1973
  • *Keep In Step With The Spirit* by J. I. Packer, Fleming H. Revell,
    1984
  • *The Practice of the Presence of God* by Brother Lawrence,
    Fleming H. Revell, 1958
  • *Man: The Dwelling Place of God* by A.W. Tozer, Christian
    Publications, 1966
  • *Enjoying Intimacy With God* by J. Oswald Sanders, Moody Press,
    1980

CHAPTER EIGHT

WHO IS GOD?

Now that we've examined sin, salvation, and spiritual growth, it's time to back up and talk about God himself. Understanding more about God is basic to other issues we will discuss, like the Bible, the church, and the Holy Spirit.

God is personal

In America, just about everyone believes God exists, but plenty of people are confused about what kind of God is there. I will assume people agree on the basic issue of God's existence and will focus instead on the issue of God's nature as a personal God.

To illustrate the confusion I'm talking about, I'll recall a conversation I had with a non-Christian. This person told me he had been discovering God in himself more and more lately. I asked how he had been seeing this and he told me, "I've just started taking a good look inside. He's been there all along!"

So I asked him to explain more about what kind of God is there. He replied that God is like a power to help you in life. "It's like a strength you can draw on to help you through." It became clear to me that this guy was thinking about God as some kind of positive force that animated things and people. I asked him if God was like a life-force and he agreed with that imagery.

This picture of God as a positive force in the world is extremely popular. A God like this is non-threatening. It's also a challenging notion to understand this God and to get on the same wavelength as him. Some people even feel that they will get some kind of power if they get in tune with God. They mistakenly believe that this view of

107

God is compatible with the Bible's view, which we'll discuss in a moment.

But there is another misconception about God that continues to be popular. Take, for example, Bette Midler's pop hit called "From a Distance" which I'm sure must have made people feel good somehow. It was about that "dear old man" in the sky who lovingly takes care of us but from a distance. In day-to-day life, you're on your own. If you really get in trouble and call out loudly enough, he might hear you and come to your aid. This view of God has been called "Deism," which means that a person believes in God, but he is so distant and uninvolved he might as well be on another planet. Again, this impression of God is not from the Bible.

First of all, the Bible insists on the personal nature of God. It would not be correct, according to the Bible, to say that God is some kind of force that lives inside us. Let's think of some of the passages that illustrate God's personality.

Exodus 34:14 tells us that God is a jealous God. He does not tolerate other impostor-gods. This jealousy is not the self-centered jealousy you or I have. God's jealousy is aroused because people promote false gods and lead others astray from the real God, which ultimately winds up in disaster for them. God's jealousy is a feeling of urgent anger because false gods ruin us spiritually. God has feelings. He is affected by our behavior. A "force" would not have this emotional reaction toward us.

Psalm 78:40 also tells us that God is grieved at times. The Israelites made God sad by the way they rejected him. When Jesus was on the earth as God in the flesh, he wept on many occasions (John 11:35; Luke 19:41). A "force" does not cry. This is the reaction of a God who is relational. How people relate to God affects him. We affect his feelings. We affect his thoughts.

Most obviously, the Bible speaks of God as "loving." Love involves many emotions. It involves free choice to love or not to love. It involves personal interaction, as love is something you *do*. The Bible speaks of God's "tender mercies" toward us. John actually personifies God as love John sees love as the most outstanding element of God's character.

And so we know and rely on the love God has for us (Luke 1:78).

God is love. Whoever lives in love lives in God, and God in him (1 John 4:16).

It would not be right at all, according to the Bible, to characterize God as some kind of force that pervades the universe. God is personal, and he is the source of our personalness. Ironically, some of the same people who think God is a kind of force also believe that he is loving. I'm not sure how this works, but maybe it has something to do with their view of love.

Now I want to digress for just a moment and consider something people frequently say about God and religion. We can demonstrate that God is personal according to the Bible, and someone might respond, "That's good for you, but I don't see God that way." People talk this way because they believe we're all ultimately talking about the same thing.

Remember the popular illustration of the blind men feeling an elephant? One blind man feels the side and says, "Elephants are like giant furry walls!" Another feels the tail and says, "No! Elephants are like rough rope!" Yet another blind man feels the legs and concludes, "Elephants are like the trunk of a tree!" People conclude from this illustration that everyone is right and it is just a matter of which part of the elephant they are talking about.

There are some serious problems with comparing our discussion of God's nature to the illustration of the blind men. We're not talking about some small facet of God's nature. We're talking about his very essence—what he *is*. To use the elephant illustration as an example, we're not discussing whether elephants have trunks or tails. We're talking about whether the elephant is alive or dead. We're talking about whether the elephant is an animal or a plant. When we talk about God's nature, we're talking about what the elephant is as a whole.

In that light, those who say God is a force are contradicting the idea that God is personal. In other words, they are saying the opposite. The Bible asserts, "God is personal. He relates to us and to himself, he is saddened, he thinks and plans." Other people are saying, "God is *not* personal. God is an *it*. God is a force."

"God is personal" versus "God is not personal" are two contradictory statements. One may be true. Or they both may be false. But they are not both true! This is a way of reasoning that is basic to human thinking. We reason this way all the time. One person could say, "The President is in the next room." Another could say, "The President is not in the next room, he's in France!" We know one or both of these people are wrong. They cannot both be right.

But something strange happens when we start talking about God. People think that the same rules of reasoning don't apply anymore.

What makes sense in day-to-day life doesn't pertain to discussions about God or the supernatural. Listen to another conversation I had not too long ago.

"Not everyone can be right about God," I said.

"Why not? People just have different views, they're not wrong," my friend objected.

"Well, if we all had different views about who you are or where you live or what kind of car you drive, you'd say, 'I am what I am! I live where I live! It doesn't matter what you guys think.'"

"Yeah, but that's me," he said. "We can talk to me, look at where I live, and see what kind of car I drive."

"That's not the point," I answered. "The point is that you are a real person, and what people *think* about you or *believe* about you doesn't change who you are. It's the same with God. No matter how hard I may believe something about him, he will still be who he is. And if people believe contradictory things about God, then either someone or everyone is wrong!"

As it turned out, my friend's main concern was how they would ever find out who was right and who was wrong. That is a great question. And it's a question we can work with. When someone is at the point where they recognize that not everyone can be right about God, then we can talk about how to find out the truth about God. We can talk about evidence for one point of view or another. But the issue to establish first is that when different points of view about God contradict each other, they cannot all be true.

Why believe that God is personal?

To what extent are we personal? Let me reclarify what I mean by "personal." I am referring to concepts like free will. A being with free will is more than just a program of chemicals and memories. A being with free will is unpredictable. They can choose something new for previously unknown reasons. They can be arbitrary. They can make choices based on intangibles like meaning or significance.

By personal, I also mean relational. We believe in the power of love, for example. Most people believe love is more than just the urges of our glands at work. Love is more than chemicals, stimulated by a drive to reproduce. Love is two personal beings who want to share each other's uniqueness. They get to know each other. They make a difference in each other's lives. They mean something to each other.

Where did these elements of personalness come from? Where did the human race inherit these characteristics? Real free will, for example, couldn't have evolved. If it is just the function of various chemical reactions, then it is essentially a program. No matter how complex a program, it is still a program. If we understood how the chemical reactions work, then we could accurately predict how a human would respond and the choices he or she would make. It's the same with love and significance. If these concepts merely originate from a higher state of chemical complexity than the animals, then we should not deceive ourselves. We should see these sentiments for what they are—chemical reactions somewhere in our bodies.

If, on the other hand, we have genuine personalness, then the most reasonable explanation is that we received it from another personal source. If the source of this world and of all human existence is personal, then it makes sense to find personal beings in creation.

I am certainly not claiming that this way of reasoning is airtight, but it does make sense. When we look at human nature, it is logical to believe that there is a source for some of the things we see.

A personal God would communicate

Here is a very important point: If it is true that God is a personal being, then that means he is a *communicating* being. Personal beings communicate. That's how we convey our individuality. The verbal and nonverbal communication we constantly project to others is the most obvious evidence of human personality.

If God exists and he is personal, then it makes sense that he would communicate. Of course he could choose not to. But I think it would be very strange to think of a personal God overseeing a creation full of personal beings and never saying a word. He never says anything about who he is? Who we are? What the meaning of this life is? I think we should behave as any scientist would. We should assume (theorize) the most likely thing, that a personal God has communicated. If we knew that intelligent life existed on other planets, were capable of sending us a message, and knew we were here, we could assume they have communicated. We should assume the same with a personal God. Now we should go out and look for that communication.

This is where the Bible comes in. The Bible claims to be a communication from God. Consider one of the clearest passages in the Bible on the topic of the Bible itself:

> All Scripture is God-breathed and is useful for teaching, rebuking, correcting and training in righteousness . . . (2 Timothy 3:16).

Paul, the author of the epistles of Timothy, asserts that all the Scriptures are "breathed from God." This is a descriptive way of saying God was involved in the writing of the Scriptures. Some other translations use the term "inspired." The New International Version is the best translation of this verse because the English term "inspired" can mean simply "enlivened" or "animated." I could have an "inspired conversation" with someone, which would mean I had a good feeling about it. I could play an inspired game of basketball, which would mean it was spirited and energetic.

But the term in 2 Timothy 3:16 means much more than "enlivened" or "animated." "God-breathed" is actually a literal translation of the term *theópneustos*. *Theo* is the Greek word for "God," and *pneustos* is a form of the Greek term for "breath." Together, these terms form a very active adjective—a term that describes God's active role in the composition of the Scriptures.

Another important point about 2 Timothy 3:16 is that it does not say, "The authors of scripture were inspired." If Paul had said that, then we could get the impression the authors felt some kind of feeling or were in an inspired state of mind. That would focus on the psychological state of the authors of the Bible. The authors of the Bible may have felt inspired as they wrote. This passage, however, focuses on the Bible itself. It focuses on the text. Paul is saying the final form, the text of the Bible, is "God-breathed."

The long and short of it all is that when we open the Bible, it claims to be from God himself. While everyone may not accept that claim as true, I'm just making the point that the Bible asserts that level of authority for itself. Some other passages where the Bible claims to be from God include 1 Corinthians 14:37:

> If anyone thinks he is a prophet or spiritual, let him recognize that the things which I write to you are the Lord's commandment.

Or we could look at Peter's appraisal of both the source and interpretation of scripture in 2 Peter 1:20–21:

> But know this first of all, that no prophecy of Scripture is a matter of one's own interpretation, for no prophecy was ever made by an act of human will, but men moved by the Holy Spirit spoke from God (NASB).

Here again is the Bible claiming to be from God to us. If we are looking for a communication from a personal God, here is at least one candidate. How many other candidates are there? Surprisingly, few. Islam claims the Qu'ran is from God, transmitted through the prophet Mohammed. Specific sects, like the Mormons with their *Book of Mormon* claim to have an inspired text. The interesting thing about both of these examples is that they trace their roots to the Bible. The Qu'ran, for example, doesn't claim to take the place of the Bible (although Islam does reject the New Testament). It claims to be an extension of biblical revelation. Likewise the *Book of Mormon* claims to be an inspired book in addition to the Bible.

What about the writings of eastern religions, such as Hinduism and Buddhism? Writings like the Baghavad Ghita or the Upanishads are associated with these religions. Here we are dealing with something different. These writings don't claim to be the revelation of a personal God. They claim to offer spiritual insight and wisdom. They are reflections on the nature of reality. But by definition they are not a communication from a personal God because neither Hinduism nor Buddhism, in all their varied forms, hold that God is a distinct, personal individual who communicates. Therefore, God is a force or an essence in the universe that we discover. The writings of these religions are the reflections of those who believe they have become more enlightened about God and ultimate reality.

So we are left with the Bible and those books which stem from the Bible. At the very least, a person who wants to seek God should look here. It is the first of all books that claim to be a personal communication from God. We should look into the Bible and see if it is a communication from God. We should look to see if it gives us any substantiating evidence. We should see if it contradicts itself. We should see if it gives us the kind of wisdom and insight we would expect in a book from God.

Study summary

Key Points
- God is personal, meaning that he communicates, has emotions, plans, and attributes of personality. All these elements of personalness can be seen in the Scriptures about God.
- The evidence for God's personalness is in creation itself. We see evidence of intelligence, design, purpose, and significance in the universe. We also see the imprint of God's personalness on ourselves.
- It is reasonable to assume that a personal God would communicate with the personal beings he has created. We should look for that communication.
- There are actually very few writings which claim to be a

communication from a personal God. The Bible was the first. Others, like the Islamic Qu'ran, came later, but also claim the Bible as a source of their authority. At the very least, we ought to first investigate the claims of the Bible to be God's Word.

Key Scriptures
- 1 John 4:16
- 2 Timothy 3:16
- 2 Peter 1:20–21

Important Terms
- Personal God
  The being who is the source of all things, yet is personal like we are. God is completely different from us in the sense that he is infinite, he depends on nothing, he is perfect. But we have personalness in common, meaning that we can communicate, love, plan, and have meaning.

- Inspiration
  When applied to the Bible, God's active participation in the creation of the text of the Scriptures. The term is taken from 2 Timothy 3:16 and is translated "God-breathed" by the New International Version, which conveys more of a sense of God's involvement in the conception of the text.

For Further Reading
- *The God Who Is There* by Francis Schaeffer, InterVarsity Press, 1968
- *He Is There and He Is Not Silent* by Francis Schaeffer, Tyndale House, 1972
- *Your God Is Too Small* by J. B. Phillips, Macmillan, 1961
- *Scaling the Secular City* by J. P. Moreland, Baker, 1987

CHAPTER NINE

THE BIBLE AS GOD'S WORD

Evidences that the Bible is what it claims to be

We have already discussed the Bible's claim to be a communication from God himself. I want to repeat that this claim is important *only if God exists and he is personal.* If God is not a personal, communicating being, then who cares about a book that claims to be from him? If someone is doubting whether the Bible could be "God's Word," then often the reason is they are not persuaded that a personal, communicating God exists.

For those who do believe a personal God exists, we can talk about the evidences that the Bible gives for itself as a communication from God. There are two primary lines of evidence the Bible gives for its own authority: prophecy and wisdom.

Prophecy

There are many prophecies in the Bible. But the type of prophecy we are interested in is the type that has already come true—fulfilled prophecy. The Bible gives these types of prophecies for the expressed purpose of validating its writings. For example, in Isaiah records this series of statements from God:

> I am the Lord; that is my name! I will not give my glory to another or my praise to idols. See, the former things have taken place, and new things I declare; before they spring into being I announce them to you (Isa. 42:8–9).

In this passage God is addressing the Israelites about their worship of other false gods. He reasons with them by giving them proof that he alone is God. The proof he gives is his unique ability to predict things before they happen. There are other passages where God uses this same reasoning (see Isa. 41:21–29).

Just as you are thinking about other prophets and writers who also predict the future, you should know that God's standards for accuracy are very high. God says that if a prophet is genuine, then his predictions will be 100% accurate. God does not make mistakes. If predictions are from God and yet mistaken, what would that say about God?

So God sets a standard to judge by—a standard that sets him apart from all other prophets. In Deuteronomy 18:21–22, he says:

> You may say to yourselves, "How can we know when a message has not been spoken by the LORD?" If what a prophet proclaims in the name of the LORD does not take place or come true, that is a message the LORD has not spoken. That prophet has spoken presumptuously. Do not be afraid of him.

In order to qualify as God's prophet, you had to be right *all the time*. Today there are readers and prophets who boast if they're right even once! That's simply not enough to claim divine inspiration. God doesn't get it wrong.

For examples of some remarkable biblical prophecies that have already come true, I will suggest some reading: *The Last Days Handbook* by Robert P. Lightner; *A Guide to Biblical Prophecy* edited by Carl E. Armerdin and Ward Gasque; and a perennial favorite, *Evidence That Demands a Verdict* by Josh McDowell.

Wisdom

Another evidence the Bible offers for itself is that it has answers. It has better answers to the real questions of life than anyone else has. It answers the questions people really struggle with. How can I fix my broken marriage? How can I forgive someone I hate? How can I ever amount to anything?

Many passages in the Bible promise that if we listen and live by its words, we will change for the better. Jesus claimed his words were the key to freedom.

> Jesus therefore was saying to those Jews who had believed Him, "If you abide in My word, then you are truly disciples of Mine; and you shall know the truth, and the truth shall make you free" (John 8:31–32).

Hebrews claims that God's Word is like a scalpel, cutting and getting to the heart of issues. Hebrews 4:12 says:

> For the word of God is living and active. Sharper than any double-edged sword, it penetrates even to dividing soul and spirit, joints and marrow; it judges the thoughts and attitudes of the heart.

Over and over again, the words of scripture demonstrate this kind of sharpness. I can't take you through a study of the Bible's wisdom here. But I challenge you to get involved in some regular Bible teaching and see if it isn't as life-changing and piercing as it claims to be.

I remember my own experience with the Bible as a young Christian. I started going to Bible studies on Wednesday night. Most of the people there were in their thirties or forties, but I was seventeen, long-haired, and driving a fifty-dollar car. Very few people that shared my interests or lifestyle. Yet the Bible teaching was attractive. I remember that it was from the book of Matthew. Each week the teacher would take a few verses from the book and explain them with applications for our lives. Even though I was not a very studious person at the time, I came every week and took notes. I had never heard so much fascinating information—so much insight into people.

That experience fed my hunger for more. I started attending Bible studies several times a week. Clearly it was no fad; it's been going on for about twelve years now and I'm still learning things every time I study the Bible.

More evidence for the Bible

There is another type of evidence for the Bible's authority that comes from examining it as a critical observer. It is the Bible's internal consistency and the way it correlates with history, geography, and science.

People have often been amazed at how the entire Bible fits together. Here is a book by dozens of authors over at least a thousand years, but it fits together as one book. I have heard from some that the Bible is "full of contradictions." It's often stated as something "everybody knows." So I'll ask for an example of one of these common contradictions. More often than not, I'll hear, "I don't know any off-hand, but I've heard there are lots of them."

I don't want to pretend I have never found any problems in the Bible. In fact, over the years I have found some very challenging propositions and apparent contradictions. Yet I have studied these passages and most of my questions have been answered very satisfactorily. There are remaining questions I have about the Bible, and I think of more questions almost every time I study it. I have good reason to believe there will be answers for these as well.

I remember being bothered by the Bible's account of the creation of the world in Genesis 1 and 2. The notion of God creating is not a problem for me at all. Some people may have a problem with the idea of God creating. Perhaps they should investigate the various arguments for the existence of God in addition to Bible study.

It appears to take place in seven days and nights. Yet when we study the geological record, it appears that the world has been billions of years in the making. So here is a seeming contradiction between the Bible and science. It is one that has bothered a lot of people too.

In my own studies, I have come to the conclusion that I had been mistakenly reading my whole world view into this ancient text. I saw the sentence, "The earth was formless and void (Gen. 1:2)," and I had this mental picture of a sphere swirling around without a distinct land-mass yet. But that's me, a twentieth-century man who has seen pictures of gaseous planets like Jupiter. I had to put myself in the shoes of a Jewish believer one thousand years before Christ. What did he think of when he read those words? What did the author intend?

The Genesis story is not primarily intended to be a description of how God created the universe, land, ocean, or any of the things we are typically interested in. It was written by Moses to Israelites to explain their relationship to God. It was kind of a preface to the rest of the books Moses wrote, known as the "Law of Moses." So the creation story of Genesis 1 is not so much concerned with the world's beginning as it is with how God prepared the world for his people. It is describing how God especially carved out a niche for humans.

When it comes to creating the world and the universe, that is all dealt with in the first verse: "In the beginning, God created the heavens and the earth." Here is the Bible's account of God creating the world and the universe. In one line it is dispatched, "In the beginning, God created the heavens and the earth." From there, Moses goes on to talk about how God prepared a world—which had already been created—for human habitation.

Looking at Genesis 1 from this perspective, there are some great insights about our place in the world. This chapter is instructive on the topic of human nature, our purpose on the planet, and our relationship to God. That's what Moses wanted to teach.

When I take the time to look into a passage that seems to be at odds with history or science, I find great answers. I see this as evidence that the Bible is a very credible word from God.

It's the same with apparent contradictions in the Bible. When I study them, I find the contradiction is only apparent, often the result of a hasty misreading of the text. I wouldn't be honest if I didn't say some passages in the Bible still puzzle me, maybe even bother me a little. But they are "little" bothers. At this stage in my studies I have been able to find great answers to my most troubling questions. I believe I will also find solutions to some of the smaller issues I come across. The Bible's record is far too good to lose sleep over.

If you are interested in getting answers to questions you have about the Bible's credibility, I refer you to two sources in particular: *The Bible Difficulty Handbook* by Gleason Archer and *Scripture and Truth* edited by Don Carson and John Woodbridge.

How much authority?

How can the Bible be God's Word when we know humans wrote it? This question is especially important when we start talking about the possibility of errors in the Bible.

The real question here is not, "How capable are humans of communicating God's word?" The real question is, "How capable is God of getting his word through to us?" Could God use humans to communicate? Could God use a machine? Could God write in the sky? The real question turns on how capable God is.

I've heard the illustration that God can use a crooked stick to draw a straight line. He is certainly able to use mistake-prone humans to write a book that accurately conveys his message. This is why the issue of God's existence and his nature are so crucial to the discussion of the Bible.

The interaction of humans and God in Scripture

Just how does God inspire his written message without turning the human authors into dictation machines? If we call the Bible "God's Word," does that mean it isn't Paul's word? Or Matthew's word?

This is a tough question. The phenomenon of prophecy may help us to better understand this interaction between God and human authors. Prophecy is a spiritual gift listed in 1 Corinthians 12:10, 28. Spiritual gifts occur when God enables a Christian to serve others in some way. God's Spirit empowers us to teach, to serve, to encourage. When this happens, he has "gifted" us.

Paul elaborates further on the nature of prophecy in 1 Corinthians 14. As I have come to understand it, prophecy is not some kind of trance where someone pronounces, "Thus saith the Lord . . ." Prophecy begins with a burden from God. It may be a burden to speak to the group about evangelism. Or it may be a strong feeling that people in the group need encouragement. As Paul says in 1 Corinthians 14:3:

> But everyone who prophesies speaks to men for their strengthening, encouragement and comfort.

So, here I am, sitting in a meeting and I have the sense God wants me to share a word of encouragement—maybe that we need to be more bold in sharing Christ. I speak up, sharing my thoughts of encouragement with people. The leading or initiation was with God, but the ideas, examples, and words were from me. They were my words of encouragement showing my personality.

As I see it, this is more or less what has happened with Scripture, with one important difference. In the case of Scripture, God went a step further and insured that what the authors wrote was in fact accurate and authoritative in every way. When I share a burden with the church, it may have all kinds of inaccuracies or exaggerations. That's the way I am. This is why Paul told us to always evaluate what a prophet says in our meetings (1 Corinthians 14:29). Even though a burden may be from God, we may be imbalanced in the way we convey it. With the authors of Scripture, however, God protected them from human imbalance or error. He was more involved, not only with giving them a burden to write, but in the final piece of communication—the text.

This is how I understand that the Scriptures can have a human author yet still be "God's Word." As we saw in 2 Timothy 3:16, the Scriptures are "inspired" or "God-breathed," as the term is rendered in the *New International Version.* This means that God is ultimately responsible for the text of the Scriptures. We also know that God is all-wise (Psalm 147:5) and cannot lie (Heb. 6:18; Titus 1:2). So, we conclude that the text of the Scriptures, which he inspired, is also free from errors. This teaching is often called "inerrancy" because it was most clearly defined in the face of much criticism about the Bible.

Study summary

Key Points
- God gives evidence for the Bible as his revealed Word. The evidence includes prophecy, which must be 100% accurate, and wisdom about life—answers that God alone has.
- The Bible has also proved to be incredibly consistent and

accurate. In spite of centuries of criticism, we find the Bible still historically reliable and internally consistent.

- God used humans to reveal his Word but that does not mean that the Bible is innately flawed. God, if he is truly God, has the power to use flawed humans to accurately reveal his Word.

Key Scriptures
- Isaiah 42:8–9
- Hebrews 4:12

Important Terms
- Prophecy
  The writings of the prophets in the Old Testament. These prophets were subject to the standard of 100% accuracy in those predictions which could be verified. They are a source of support for the claim that the Bible is given by God.

  The New Testament practice of allowing God to address the needs of others through us. In the church, prophecy is much different from the authoritative oracles of the Old Testament prophets. It is simply when God uses our words to uplift, encourage, or even expose others in the church.

- Inerrancy
  The teaching that God inspired the text of the Scriptures, and it is therefore free from mistakes and errors. In response to much criticism over the reliability of the text of Scripture, many Christians have defined their position on the authority of Scripture by using this term.

For Further Reading
- *Scripture and Truth* edited by D. A. Carson and John Woodbridge, Zondervan, 1983
- *The Bible: Breathed From God* by Robert L. Saucy, Victor Books, 1980
- *Inerrancy* edited by Norman Geisler, Zondervan, 1980
- *How to Read the Bible For All It's Worth* by Gordon Fee and Douglas Stewart, Zondervan, 1982
- *Handbook for Bible Study* by Grant R. Osborne and Stephen B. Woodward, Baker, 1979

CHAPTER TEN

THE CHURCH

Misconceptions about the church

I won't surprise anyone when I say that many people don't like the church. For those who have had a positive experience in the church, this may be hard to understand. But we have to realize that some people have really suffered at the hands of those who call themselves Christians.

Just this week I was watching an exposé on a televangelist who had ripped off millions of dollars using standard marketing techniques. The followers who lost their money were obviously disillusioned, but so were the millions who tuned in to that program!

Some Christians will object, saying that the disreputable televangelists have nothing to do with the church. But that is not the impression the average person has. The average non-Christian remembers every negative image of Christians. And there are enough out there to turn anyone sour.

I don't believe for one minute that the church is unattractive. I believe Christ's church is the single best thing going on the face of the earth! There is no comparison to any other movement, institution, event, or group of people. The problem is that there are corrupt institutions calling themselves the church, people who claim an exclusive right to Christ's church, and countless counterfeits of the church.

So the first thing we'll do in our study of the church is to discuss what the church is not. We'll look at popular misconceptions of the church.

An institution

The boards, the hierarchies, the rules, the politics, all the trappings of big business are what a lot of people think of when they think of the church. Many Roman Catholics have an indelible impression of the church as an everlasting institution with popes and bishops and councils.

Protestants also have their traditions and institutions. If you've been raised in an established church, chances are you have even taken classes on how great your denomination is. Many churches pride themselves on what a great network of programs they have built, what a great building they have, and what a great institution they are.

The church is not an institution! The church may spawn many institutions as a family may build houses. They may be great ones. But the church is not an institution.

A building

The most common misconception of the church is simply that of a building. People think, "I'll go down to the church," and they have in mind a building on the corner. This is an innocent enough mistake. We all call the buildings where the church meets "churches." But there are dangers. There is the danger that people will believe that the building is special. There is the danger that people will begin to orient the life of the church around the building rather than make building serve the life of the church.

Think of a scenario that is happening right now near you if you live in or near a big city. Downtown there are a few big churches made of stone with big, old steeples and organs. The members of this church live out in the suburbs but they drive into the city on Sunday to go to "the church." Every so often they think, "What are we doing? Our attendance is dwindling. We don't attract people from the neighborhood. And our kids hate driving down here with us!" But they won't change. They won't do anything about it. They won't move into their own neighborhoods to reach out to their friends *because of the church*! By "the church," they mean the building.

I don't know of any easy solutions for this. That's because there are none. Solutions require a great deal of faith and sacrifice. Perhaps the people of "downtown church" should go ahead and turn their church building over to the Christians who actually live in the neighborhood. Maybe they should just desert the building. Maybe they should keep it as a museum of how Christians used to worship. But the last thing they should do is try to force the life of the church into the mold of some old building!

A social club for the family

In the early 80's there was a mass return to the church by "Baby Boomers" who wanted to get their kids involved. They thought the right friends and wholesome activities would be good for them. Maybe the church can perform those functions. But that is not the essence of the church.

You don't go to MacDonalds to find a place to sit. To use the church as a place to expose your family to good company is to completely misunderstand what the church is. It's no wonder a lot of these same people soon leave the church wondering, "What do people see in that thing anyway?"

What the Bible says about the church

When we turn to the Bible, however, we find a much different picture of the church. The real church is not at all like the popular myths so many people accept.

It belongs to Christ.

When Jesus had spent years with his disciples, he began to talk to them about the church. They didn't understand fully what he was about to do, but he talked about it anyway. One of the things he said was to Peter in Matthew 16:18, "And I tell you that you are Peter, and on this rock I will build my church, and the gates of Hades will not overcome it."

Jesus was not saying that Peter would be the first pope. He was saying that Peter would be a foundational leader in the church. "I will use you to build my church!" was the exciting promise Christ made to him. Peter was privileged to be one of the founding apostles of the church and history tells us he paid for that privilege with his life.

The point I want to draw from this passage is that Christ calls it, "my church." And he says, "I will build it." Then, throughout the rest of the New Testament, that ownership is assumed (see 1 Cor. 3:9). I wonder how many people see it this way? I think most people conceive of denominations, institutions, and boards who run things.

To get practical about this concept, let's think of a recent decision in your church, perhaps it was a building or an addition. Maybe it was cutting a program. But on what basis did the leaders of the church make that decision? Did they search for the leadership of Jesus Christ? Or was it just the easiest way? Was it a majority opinion?

There are churches—sadly, fewer than I wish—who take the time in prayer, in searching the Scriptures, and in consulting with other wise Christians to discover God's will. But many others cynically believe that searching for Christ's leadership in the church is a superstitious relic from the past.

Another practical implication of Christ's ownership of the church is that human leadership ought to be subject to him. We would see fewer abuses of authority in the church if human leaders subjected themselves to the authority of Christ. Look at the way Paul views himself in 1 Corinthians 3:6–9:

> I planted the seed, Apollos watered it, but God made it grow. So neither he who plants nor he who waters is anything, but only God, who makes things grow. The man who plants and the man who waters have one purpose, and each will be rewarded according to his own labor. For we are God's fellow workers; you are God's field, God's building.

Paul uses the analogy of planting to describe his work in starting the church at Corinth. Notice how he disclaims any ownership, "you are God's field, God's building." And Paul's humility shows through when he says, "neither he who plants nor he who waters is anything." Imagine if today's pastors and televangelists really believed this!

It consists of all Christians.

The Bible also teaches that the church is people. The church consists of all Christians from all time. Paul, who often used the metaphor of the human body to describe the church, says this in Ephesians 4:3–6:

> Make every effort to keep the unity of the Spirit through the bond of peace. There is one body and one Spirit—just as you were called to one hope when you were called—one Lord, one faith, one baptism; one God and Father of all, who is over all and through all and in all.

Paul is trying to emphasize through repetition that all Christians are one. There is only one body (church).

There are several practical implications of this teaching. For one, if we understood all Christians are part of the church, this might help create greater unity. On the one hand, I think it is good that not all Christians are doing the same thing. The fact that there are different churches and Christian groups reflects the differences between people. It's also great to see how God can work in so many different ways. Non-Christians who would not darken the doorstep of one church might feel right at home in another.

The problem comes when one church thinks they have a corner on it all. When one group of Christians starts to think the others aren't really part of Christ's church because they aren't institutionally affiliated, then we are in error.

The only affiliation that counts is faith in Jesus Christ. This is why membership rosters can be so deceiving. They may give people the impression they are part of the church simply by being part of an institution.

The term "church" can refer to any gathering of Christians.

When we look at the big picture, the term "church," which is translated from the Greek term *ekklesia*, refers to all those who belong to Christ throughout the world and throughout history. However, the term is used in the Bible to refer to almost any type of *gathering*. In Acts 9:31 the term is used to refer to the church in the region of Judea, Galilee, and Samaria. In 1 Corinthians 1:2 it refers to the church in the city of Corinth. And in Romans 16:5 Paul refers to the church in Prisca and Aquila's house. Obviously the term "church" can refer to virtually any type of Christian gathering.

This varied use of the term "church" is why people make a distinction between the local church and the universal church. The universal church is what we have described above—all Christians throughout history. The local church refers to Christians in any geographical area who gather together (not necessarily all at once). We could talk about the church in New York or the church in New York City. We could talk about the church that meets in a particular building in New York City.

Some people would like to define the local church more strictly than this. They say the church must have memberships, or a particular type of organization or purpose. I think there is a danger, though, in defining the local church more narrowly than we have. We can begin to feel the need for certain structures, offices, or membership levels before we have a *real* church. Not only does this go beyond scriptural guidelines, it also places an undue burden on small, struggling churches.

Throughout the world, thousands of churches are planted every week. We shouldn't impose definitions on them that are unrealistic or even unbiblical. Excessively defining a local church can lead to an overly narrow view of what a legitimate church is. As a church grows it may acquire a higher degree of organization, structure, and possessions. This does not make a smaller, newer, or less-organized church any less of a church.

It is the center of God's work on earth.

The church is the most exciting thing on earth! If we see it for what it is, the church is the sum of everything God is doing on the earth. Paul tells us God's plan is to bring everything and everyone under the authority of Christ. He puts it this way in Ephesians 1:9:

> And he made known to us the mystery of his will according to his good pleasure, which he purposed in Christ, to be put into effect when the times will have reached their fulfillment—to bring all things in heaven and on earth together under one head, who is Christ.

So Paul says that the "mystery" of God's will is he is going to bring everyone under Christ's authority. How is he going to do this? Paul says later in the same chapter:

> And God placed all things under his feet and appointed him to be head over everything for the church, which is his body, the fullness of him who fills everything in every way (vv. 22–23).

Again, the church is Christ's "body." He is in charge (the "head"), but the body does the work. Paul uses a puzzling set of terms at the end of this verse: "The fullness of him who fills everything in every way." What Paul is saying is that the church is the full expression of Christ's authority. The church completely embodies Christ's work and rulership on this earth.

It's the entire church—every Christian in all of time.

To get practical, the Bible teaches us that if God is going to work in this world, he will do so through the church. If he is going to grant anyone salvation, it will come through the church. If he is going to communicate with anyone, it will come through the church. If he is going to heal anyone or minister to someone in any way, then it will be through the church. Certainly there are exceptions, times when God will intervene directly without any human agency, but on the whole, the church is Christ's body on this earth.

It takes a little time to grasp the importance of this truth. When we do, it's very, very exciting. You see, God could have worked in this world on his own. If he wanted to speak to someone, he is capable of writing a message in the sky. If he wanted to change people, God could transform them in a puff of white smoke. Instead, he works through the church, meaning he works through you and me. He has decided to do his work in this world through humans.

People say, "Why doesn't God reveal himself to me? I want him to talk to me!" He has given us the church. People say, "I want God to work a miracle in my life! I need help from God!" Again, he has given us the church. It is truly astounding that God has chosen to work this way. For one thing, wouldn't his reputation be better served if God did things himself? Incredibly, he entrusts his work to fallen and corrupt humans.

Yet, when we look closely, we see the beauty of why God has decided to work through the church in this world. By working this way, he has ensured that we will always need each other. He has guaranteed that people will have to work with each other, live with each other, go to each other to get needs met, and work out differences. In short, the way God has decided to work in this world is the basis for love.

C. S. Lewis, in his book *The Great Divorce*, envisioned a fascinating picture of hell. He described it as a place where every need is met by simply imagining. So, for example, if you wanted a house you would simply think of it. New arrivals in hell were amazed by this capacity at first. But soon they realized it meant they were completely self-sufficient. Now, other people were unnecessary. Sooner or later, everyone would get into an argument, or they would irritate each other. Eventually, everyone in hell moved away from everyone else. People who had been there for hundreds of years— the Ghengis Khans, the Napoleons—were so far gone, no one could find them.

I have no idea whether hell will be like that or not. But the insightful part of this scenario is that this world would truly be loveless if we didn't need each other. In the church, God has made our need for one another even more pronounced.

In 1 Corinthians 12, Paul again uses the metaphor of the human body to teach that each of the "parts" needs the others.

> As it is, there are many parts, but one body. The eye cannot say to the hand, "I don't need you!" And the head cannot say to the feet, "I don't need you!" (vv. 20–21).

God gives us meaningful and different roles in the church. But sometimes when there are differences, we depreciate those unlike ourselves. In this passage, Paul is warning that those very differences are what we need, just like an eye needs a foot to get around and a foot needs an eye to see where to go.

Spiritual gifts

The different roles we perform in the church are related to what the Bible calls "spiritual gifts." One passage tells us very simply what a spiritual gift is. 1 Corinthians 12:7 (NASB) says:

> But to each one is given the manifestation of the Spirit for the common good.

A spiritual gift is a "manifestation of the Spirit" according to this verse. This means when we see a spiritual gift, it is the Holy Spirit himself who is manifested. In other words, God works directly through us. When he gifts someone to speak, he speaks through that person. When he gifts someone to serve, God serves through that person.

Spiritual gifts are an exciting feature of the Christian life. To be gifted by God is to have his power work through you. And you can see from the last part of verse 7 that gifting always occurs to meet needs "for the common good," as Paul puts it. Paul goes on to list various ways God gifts people for service such as wisdom, knowledge, prophecy, healing, and more.

I've had countless people ask me what I think their spiritual gift is. This question reflects a static view of God's gifting. The fact is, God can work through us in a variety of ways. At one time he may use you to encourage someone. The next day he may use you to teach or serve. The important part is that a gift occurs when God works through you.

Of course, God takes advantage of abilities and features that are already present. If you are knowledgeable or have experience communicating, then God may work through you to teach others. Or if you have experience in life, then God may use you to give someone a word of wisdom. This is why we often see a connection between someone's spiritual gifting and their life before they became a Christian. An outgoing salesperson might be good at sharing the gospel. A good administrator might be used by God to lead.

The actual experience of God's gifting may range from something quite extraordinary to something virtually unnoticeable. Sometimes when I teach I get the distinct impression God is speaking through me. There are also times when I'm praying or thinking about things, and I get the impression God is laying a burden on my heart. Then there are other times, like when I was sitting on my porch recently and I made a few observations to a friend of mine about some positive things I'd seen in him lately. Later he told me he was very discouraged, but my words were like a reminder from God to keep going. I knew at that moment God had spoken through me without me knowing it.

We need to see these subtle but life-changing experiences as miraculous. The truth is that a miracle occurs whenever God enters into this world and works. Christians typically don't recognize miracles unless they are gross violations of the laws of nature. That's why we miss so much of what God is doing all around us. Instead of looking for the spectacular, we ought to be amazed by the everyday, intimate work of God in our lives. And we see this work every day in Christ's church.

Study summary

Key Points
* The church is not a building, an institution, or a social club.
* The church is people—all the people who have committed their life to Christ in faith.
* The church belongs to Christ, not to any organization, leader, or denomination.
* We can distinguish between the local church and the universal church. The universal church consists of all people throughout history who have trusted in Christ. The local church is any geographical subset of that group.
* The church is the center of God's work in this world. That includes his work with you and me. If we wish to have God work with us, that means getting involved with the church.
* God empowers people to serve, which is called "spiritually gifting" people. This is how God works through humans supernaturally.

Key Scriptures
* Matthew 16:18
* Ephesians 4:3–6
* 1 Corinthians 12

Important Terms
* The Church
  People from all over the world and throughout all history who belong to Christ. The church is not an institution, building, or denomination.

  Christians in a given locale who gather together. In any region, city, or even house, Christians can gather and be legitimately referred to as a church.

* The Body of Christ
  A metaphor for the church. Sometimes the Bible describes the

- Spiritual gifts
  When God empowers us to serve others. Whenever God works through us to effect others, that is a spiritual gift. He may use those talents and skills that are already present, or he may work through us in a way that is totally new.

For Further Reading
  - *Showing the Spirit* by D. A. Carson, Baker, 1987
  - *The Problem of Wineskins* by Howard Snyder, InterVarsity, 1975
  - *Body Life* by Ray Stedman, Regal Books, 1972)
  - *Sharpening the Focus of the Church* by Gene Getz, Victor Books, 1984
  - *The Church: God's People* by Bruce Shelley, Victor Books, 1978

CHAPTER ELEVEN

THE HOLY SPIRIT

When we talk about the Holy Spirit, we also need to address why the Bible describes God as more than one person. Hopefully, this will explain why it is that we have an entire section devoted to the study of God's Spirit—because he is a different person.

The Trinity

The teaching that God is three persons is called the "Trinity." There is no verse in Scripture that talks about the term "trinity." The term was coined to describe what people saw in the Bible.

From the very beginning of the Bible, God portrays himself as more than one person. In the creation story the Spirit of God appears as an active participant (Gen. 1:3). As the story goes on, God discusses the creation of human beings (see vv. 26–27). This is significant because in the course of the discussion, it becomes clear who God is talking to. First God says, "Let *us* make man in *our* image." Then, God creates Adam. And Genesis sums up, "God created man in his image." The "our image" of verse 26 is "God's image" according to verse 27.

Later God tells the Israelites, "Hear O Israel, the Lord our God, the Lord is one!" (Deut. 6:4). Probably every religious Jew has memorized this verse. It is one of the reasons they cannot conceive of either Jesus Christ or the Holy Spirit to be distinct persons who are also God. It is interesting, however, that the term the author uses at this point is not the term for the number "one." When he says that the Lord is "one," the term he selects is one that means "unity," meaning our God has "oneness." For example, the same term is used later in Genesis to describe the entire human race as "united" or "one" when they all spoke the same language (see Gen. 11:6).

I believe this is again very significant because it is in complete harmony with what we see throughout the rest of Scripture. God is three persons, but those persons are so in harmony they are one.

Later in the Bible, the teaching that God is more than one person becomes very clear. We already saw that the Bible teaches Jesus Christ is God. It is also clear that he was distinct from the Father. How else could he say on the cross, "Father, Father, why have you forsaken me?" There are many other places where Christ establishes the distinction between himself and both the Father and the Holy Spirit (see John 8:18; John 14:16–17).

Likewise, the Spirit of God is equated with God himself (see 1 Corinthians 3:17; Acts 5:3, 4). At the same time, he is distinct from both the Father and Jesus Christ (see John 14:16–17). There are other passages that talk about all three persons together such as Matthew 28:19 where Jesus tells us to baptize "in the name of the Father, the Son and the Holy Spirit." In 1 Corinthians 12:4–6 Paul again lists all three persons together as the movers and powers in the church.

Why so unclear?

It is fair to wonder why the Bible takes so long to clearly reveal the Trinity. Why didn't God just come out and say he is three persons?

One pattern we see in Scripture is God does not reveal everything at once. For example, with his plan to save the human race, he would only say that some day one of Eve's descendants would crush Satan (Gen. 3:15). Even to Abraham, he would only say that one day he would become a blessing to the whole world (Gen. 12:1–3). By the time of Christ, though, an elaborate plan of salvation unfolded. So God reveals things only as they are necessary.

On top of that, there was at least one good reason to downplay God's plurality. The Jews were coming out of a polytheistic culture. "Polytheistic" means "many gods." The cultures around them believed in a "god of this, god of that" type of religion. The Old Testament is very clearly fighting against these contemporary ideologies. As such, it makes sense for God to downplay his plurality. It could have easily been misinterpreted by many.

How does it work?

A second great question is simply, how can three be one? It's a difficult question that has often been considered an unanswerable question. I don't propose to make the teaching of the Trinity absolutely clear. But I do think we have to resist the answer that says, "Oh, well! It's God, so we'll never understand him!" That approach accepts that the biblical teaching of the Trinity is nonsensical or even contradictory. If we accept that, then it seems to me one of Christianity's greatest strengths disappears—that the Christian faith does not require you to reject your reason. Some faiths say reason and faith are not compatible. But as Christians, we not only believe they are compatible; they are complimentary.

Basically, the Christian position on the unity and diversity of the Trinity begins the same way as the teaching of Christ's dual nature— by making a distinction between God's nature and God's personhood. God's nature is everything it is to be God. We talk about "human nature" as those elements we all have in common. God's nature is whatever it is to be God. Things like infinite power, all wisdom, and unlimited love are characteristics of God's nature.

Then there is the element of personhood. Defining personhood or putting your finger on it is no easy task. It is that which makes us different. I am a human, but I am also *me*. I am unique. I have human nature the same as everyone else. But I am Scot McCallum. What is it that makes me different? What is it that makes me a unique person? Is it just the fact that I look different or have a different combination of personality traits? I don't think so. I believe there is a person, Scot McCallum, who is distinct from all other persons. And it wouldn't matter what my personality was or what I looked like.

I realize this distinction is not absolutely clear. But it's not ridiculous either. We can see the difference between someone's nature and someone's personhood. If you agree then it is possible to grasp the concept of the Trinity. The Trinity is not a matter of three persons who are also one person. The Trinity is three persons united in one divine nature.

I could go further about the unity of the Trinity because I believe we need more explanation to show why the Trinity is so unified that they are called "one." Humans, after all, share the same nature and are distinct persons. Why can't we be called "one"? Part of the answer lies in the very nature of what it is to be God. When we talk about human nature—that which we all share in common—part of it may be that we are distinct. We are all independent to some degree. But when we talk about the nature of God, it may be that part of what it is to be God is to be joined with the other members of the Trinity. They are so completely united so as to be one God.

A third point about the unity of the Trinity has to do with their communication. The three members of the Trinity are in complete and constant communication, which results in a oneness of purpose, thought, and expression. Consider, for example, the institution of marriage. In creating marriage, God declared, "the two should become one" (Gen. 2:24). As physical beings, this unity is partly sexual. But any married person will tell you that sex does not bring complete oneness. The real oneness comes from communication—how much of yourself you share with that other person. To the degree a couple is able to truly share themselves with each other, they will be one.

I believe each member of the Trinity is able to completely share himself with the others at all times. Their communication is so complete they are one.

Now, all the way through this part of the discussion I have repeated the phrase, "I believe." That's because I have no clear Scripture on this point. We have the paradigm of marriage. We know God created humans male and female. We also know he created humans in his image. So it does seem reasonable to speculate God also has a unity something like he envisioned for humans.

There is no doubt that every explanation of the Trinity is going to leave unanswered questions. The main points I want to communicate here are that 1) it is taught in the Bible, 2) it is not absurd or ridiculous to believe in the Trinity, and 3) there is some basis in our own experience to understand it.

The Holy Spirit, then, is God, and he is a person. He has voluntarily taken on certain roles that are unique to him. For example, when it comes to our relationship with God, the Holy Spirit is the one we experience firsthand. So we will look now at how the Spirit interacts with Christians.

The experience of God

The Bible teaches us when we turn to God for his forgiveness, he sends his Spirit to live inside us. This is why people who become Christians report they have a new spiritual awareness. They have a sense that they are in touch with God in a new way. Paul explains in Romans 8:9 that all Christians are indwelt by God's Spirit.

> You, however, are controlled not by the sinful nature but by the Spirit, if the Spirit of God lives in you. And if anyone does not have the Spirit of Christ, he does not belong to Christ.

Clearly, everyone who is a Christian has the Spirit of God living inside them. It may not always feel that way, but he is there. This is affirmed by the promises of Christ as well (see John 14:16–17; Acts 1:4–5).

But let's not let the biblical teaching about God's Spirit become just a few verses to know and memorize. The amazing thing about the Spirit of God is that God comes to relate to us. God comes to live with us every day, every minute of every day. We say things like, "God loves me" or "God cares." But those are just sayings. This is real substance. This is real experience. God comes to live inside us!

> And hope does not disappoint us, because God has poured out his love into our hearts by the Holy Spirit, whom he has given us (Rom. 5:5).

The whole notion of God's love is made real by the fact that he comes and lives inside us. The Holy Spirit communicates it to us. Paul puts it another way a little later in Romans.

> For you have not received a spirit of slavery leading to fear again, but you have received a spirit of adoption as sons by which we cry out, "Abba! Father!" The Spirit Himself bears witness with our spirit that we are children of God (Rom. 8:15 NASB).

The people Paul is writing to had previously been involved in spiritual religions based on fear and intimidation. Many had been involved in occult practices. So Paul is saying the Holy Spirit is not like that. Instead, he works in our hearts to assure us we have a relationship with God—a relationship so close he is like a father to us. Actually, the term "Abba" could best be translated "Dad."

Perhaps those who did not have a very close relationship with their father have a hard time appreciating this picture. But the idea is that God wants to be intimate with us. Think of someone you have had intimacy with. That is the type of relationship God wants, only closer.

Not everyone experiences God the same

As soon as I start talking about experiencing the love of God, I know that not everyone experiences God's love in the same way. In my own experience, there have been times when I knew he loved me more than anything. I have been moved to tears by the strong sense of God's love. But there have been other times I didn't feel like he even existed! Yet the Bible says at all times he is living inside me! How can this be?

The answer is that there are means or channels through which God's

Spirit works to relate with us. Paul hints at this in Romans 8, just previous to the verse we read:

> For all who are being led by the Spirit of God, these are sons of God (v. 14).

Every Christian, to one degree or another, is being led by God. I say "to one degree or another" because it is not the same for all of us. Some of us are being led by God's Spirit a lot, some a little. And this difference explains, in part, how much Christians are aware of their relationship to God—their father.

The degree to which you are led by God's Spirit explains how much awareness you have of God's love for you. It explains how much confidence you have in God's love for you. Now, what do I mean by being led by God's Spirit? Very simply this: that you are doing what he tells you. You are following him. You are listening to him.

Here is an important point. We say the Spirit is assuring us that we are God's children. We say the Spirit of God is teaching us to have a relationship with him where we view him as "Dad." The problem is that some people are drowning out this voice. Some people are listening to every other voice except the voice of God's Spirit.

I know when I was a very young Christian I struggled with this whole idea that "God loves you." It seemed to me like a pat Christian answer to our doubts and struggles. But where's the substance? What does it mean to say that God loves me? This question irritated me so much that I left the church and just quit the whole "Christian thing," convinced it was a farce.

My problem was that I was drowning out the voice of God's Spirit with drugs, with busyness, with just about everything I could. I didn't take the time to develop my relationship with God.

Many Christians need to slow down and start listening to what God's Spirit is *definitely* trying to tell them.

We have already covered the means the Spirit uses to communicate to us. When we discussed spiritual growth, we defined it as getting closer to God. It is a relational goal. And the means we pursue to get closer to God are the same ones we use to be led by God's Spirit. It is precisely the same idea.

As we discussed then, listening to God's Spirit involves letting him teach us through the Scriptures. Anyone who doesn't crack open their Bible, read it, and let the Spirit speak to them through it is not getting very close to God. Listening involves prayer. And in prayer, we should actually spend time listening. We should think through issues in our lives "in the presence of God," so to speak. Let him address you. Let him bring things to your attention.

When I say this kind of thing, I worry that people will conceive of a booming voice, like in the movies. That's not what I mean. I believe the Spirit communicates to us by thoughts, urgings, and convictions. In 1 Thessalonians 5:9, Paul teaches that God is trying to instruct us:

> Now about brotherly love we do not need to write to you, for you yourselves have been taught by God to love each other.

Notice the distinction between "someone writing to you," which would be Scripture, and the fact that the God himself can instruct us. What Paul is describing is a common scenario. Let's say there is a person in your life you know you should be loving. It could be a family member, a roommate, a friend. You will begin to get the sense that you ought to be doing something. "I ought to sit down and find out what's really happening lately." "I ought to say something positive." "I ought to share myself more with her."

That could very well be God trying to teach you—trying to lead you. If you are taking time to pray and listen to God, you will get a lot of these impressions. He will teach you practical ways to love.

Now I would caution that we don't need to go around insisting that the various impressions we have are, in fact, from God. I say this because the truth is, we never know for sure. The only word from God we know for sure is the Bible. The impression we have may be from God or it may be from our own heads. There is no way to say positively. So, I do two things:

I avoid calling my impressions "God's voice" or anything like that to others. The reason I do this is because people may take me too seriously. In some Christian circles it's commonplace to go around saying, "God told me this and that." When we say, "God told me," it has such an air of authority. It has such a sound of importance. But the fact is, we aren't sure! We can never be sure. Why attach such an importance to something we can't be sure about? I think it's dangerous.

Secondly, when it comes to things I believe God has revealed to me, I always try to compare it with the Bible. I know if something I feel a conviction about is at odds with the Scriptures, then it wasn't God. Now this step may take a good degree of Bible knowledge. Some of us don't have that level of knowledge about the Bible yet. In the meantime, we could talk about the things we're thinking with other Christians. Bounce your thoughts off other Christians who know the Scriptures and hear what they say. It's always a good idea to do this.

Finally, the Spirit also leads us through the work and words of other Christians, as I discussed in the chapter on the church. How many times have you been at a Bible study, for example, and realized God was working through that teacher to speak to you? Or how many times have I been talking to a friend who begins to speak to me about some area of concern in my life and I realize, "I'd better listen to this because it sounds like godly wisdom"? It happens quite a bit and it reaffirms that God is at work in my life. God has also worked through Christian authors to speak to me.

God can use virtually any means to lead us: events, suffering, family, bosses, and co-workers. Often young Christians are eager to interpret things that happen to them as "signs from God." I don't think those of us who are older and cynical should scoff at this attitude. This is a practical application of a passage like Romans 8:28, "God works all things together for good for those who love him and are called according to his purpose." If God is truly working behind the scenes in all things, we should desire to be sensitive to him.

Empowering

Another role the Spirit performs in our lives is what we could call "empowering." The Spirit gives us power to do God's will. It's not enough for him to show us what to do. We would still be incapable of doing it.

For years I've been struggling with the issue of being more positive with people. What comes naturally to me is negativity, sarcasm, criticism. I know this is contrary to love. And I know God wants me to have victory in this area. But my negative ways are so automatic, I feel I can't stop! I feel so frustrated after I come home at night and realize most of my relating with people was, once again, negative.

This is where the power of God's Spirit comes to our aid. He wants to enable us to change. And he wants that change to be real, from the inside out, not just cosmetic. The truth is, I could probably curb my negativity to some degree in some settings. We all know what it's like to desperately grasp for control of our sins in one setting, only to have them burst out in another—often upon our own families.

So God's Spirit is the key to change that is not just superficial. He alone has the ability to change even the way we think. As Paul describes in Romans 12:2, God can "renew our minds." But what is required for this empowering is a certain level of neediness, a certain degree of hunger. We have to want him to work within us. The drive to handle things ourselves, the fear of turning our lives over to God, prevents us from depending on the Spirit to work.

I'm one who has always had a hard time with the idea of "depending on God." It bothers me when people say, "You just need to really depend on God here." What does that mean? Am I supposed to do anything? Am I supposed to try?

This attitude of hunger is key to understanding dependence. There has to be a sense of my own weakness. And when that awareness is present, we turn to the Spirit for empowering. As God told Paul in 2 Corinthians 12:9a:

> My grace is sufficient for you, for power is perfected in weakness (NASB).

We've talked much about the attitude of faith so I don't want to belabor the point here. I just want to make clear that the Spirit's empowering is there for those who really want it.

The filling of the Spirit

We should conclude this discussion of the Holy Spirit with some thoughts about being "filled with the Spirit." Basically, to be filled with the Spirit is to be empowered by the Spirit. But it is such a popular phrase with Christians we should try to understand it better.

Being filled with the Spirit appears to be a popular term for the early Christians as well. It comes up ten times in the book of Acts, and also in Paul's letters. In Acts, there are two basic ways the phrase is used. First, it is used as a description of mature Christian character (see Acts 6:5; 11:24). To say someone is "full of the Spirit" for Luke was to say that the Holy Spirit was in charge, the Spirit had really changed that person.

Secondly, the phrase is used to describe someone who was serving God. It may have been preaching the gospel (Acts 4:8) or performing a miracle (Acts 13:9). But the phrase is consistently used in the context of the Lord's service. This is why I said being filled with the Spirit is the same notion as empowering. It happens when we let the Holy Spirit take charge and speak through us or help us to serve someone.

It's exciting to talk to a young Christian after their first experience of being filled with the Spirit. Recently a friend of mine was talking to one of his non-Christian friends and he had this experience. "I felt like I was saying things that I never even knew before!" he told me.

He felt he had persuasive wisdom from God way beyond his abilities. It's a powerful experience. And it is one we should actually seek out, asking God to fill us with his Spirit. Paul, in fact, commands us to seek out this experience in Ephesians 5:18:

> And do not get drunk with wine, for that is dissipation, but be filled with the Spirit (NASB).

Then Paul goes on to explain that being filled with the Spirit involves "speaking to one another in Psalms, hymns and spiritual songs" (v. 19). So, it is in the context of serving others, speaking for God, and sharing the gospel we are filled with the Spirit.

I talk to Christians all the time who don't have the experience of God's Spirit. At the same time, they never try to serve anyone or share the message of Christ with anyone. That's where we'll experience this empowering. So I recommend we pray to God, "God, show me where I can be used by your Spirit. Show me someone I can share Christ with. Show me someone I can encourage with the power of your Spirit." And then look for an opportunity because that is a prayer God will answer.

Study summary

Key Points
- The Holy Spirit is God, the third member of the Trinity.
- The Trinity is a concept that gradually unfolds in the Bible, probably because God didn't want people to think in the polytheistic terms of their contemporary culture.
- The basic teaching of the Trinity is three persons who are united in one nature as God.
- One example of how this might work is the human relationship of marriage. When God created humans male and female, he expressed the ideal that "the two should become one." Surely all such parallels fall short of the way it actually works with God, however.
- All Christians have God's Spirit living within them.
- The Holy Spirit is how we actually experience God's presence, his love and his guidance.
- We can short-circuit our experience of the Holy Spirit by ignoring him, by sin, or simply failing to work on our relationship with God.
- The Spirit gives us power to grow spiritually and serve others. This is called the "filling of the Spirit."

Key Scriptures
- 1 Corinthians 3:17
- 1 Corinthians 12:4–6
- Matthew 28:18–20
- Romans 8:9
- John 14:16–17
- Romans 8:14–15
- Ephesians 5:18

Important Terms
- The Trinity
  Three distinct persons who are all God. All three persons, the Father, the Son, and the Holy Spirit, have one nature—Deity.

- The Holy Spirit
  A third distinct person who is also God. The Spirit of God is not a part of God the Father; he is distinct from both Jesus and the Father. He is the member of the Trinity who comes to live inside of us and therefore the one we experience on a regular basis.

- Leading
  In the context of the Holy Spirit, when he teaches and guides us. He can do this through others, the Scriptures, or through more personal communication like visions, revelations, or simply a sense of divine guidance.

- Empowering
  In the context of the Holy Spirit, when he enables us to serve others. The empowering of the Spirit is very much the same as spiritual gifting. He can empower us to share our faith, teach others, love.

- Filling
  Another term for the empowering of the Spirit. The term is used most often in connection with sharing the gospel or speaking out for Christ.

  As an adjective, to be "Spirit-filled" means to be generally in submission to God's Spirit. Sometimes the term is used in a more general sense to describe the overall character of a person's life. In this context, to be "Spirit-filled" means that you let the Holy Spirit have his way with you.

For Further Reading
- *Understanding the Trinity* by Alister McGrath, Zondervan, 1988
- *Baptism and Fullness* by John R. W. Stott, InterVarsity, 1975